Food for Friends

Food for Friends

homemade gifts for every season

SALLY PASLEY VARGAS

photography by CAROLINE KOPP

TEN SPEED PRESS
Berkeley | Toronto

For Luke,
the most precious gift of all.

Ten Speed Press
PO Box 7123
Berkeley, California 94707
www.tenspeed.com

Distributed in Australia by Simon and Schuster Australia, in Canada by Ten Speed Press Canada, in New Zealand by Southern Publishers Group, in South Africa by Real Books, and in the United Kingdom and Europe by Airlift Book Company.

Project Management by Holly Taines White
Editorial Management by Andrea Chesman
Cover and Text Design by Toni Tajima
Food and Prop Styling by Wesley Martin, San Francisco
Hand Modeling by Camella Haecker
Additional Modeling by Elaine Lissner
Props provided by Sur la Table, 77 Maiden Lane, San Francisco, California, 94108; (415) 732-7900;
    www.surlatable.com
Special thanks to Angela Oliva for the use of her backyard.

Library of Congress Cataloging-in-Publication Data
Vargas, Sally Pasley.
Food for friends : homemade gifts for every season / Sally Pasley Vargas.
p. cm.
ISBN 1-58008-056-1 (pbk.)
1. Cookery. 2. Gifts. I. Title.
TX652 .V373   2000
641.5—dc21   00-037794

First printing, 2000
Printed in Hong Kong

6 7 8 9 10 — 07 06 05 04 03

contents

Acknowledgments

No woman is an island, least of all, one who writes a cookbook. Grandmothers, friends, mentors, and a world of cookbook authors stand at her elbow and whisper in her ear, in person and in spirit, guiding her every step. How I came to be so rich in friends is a mystery, but I am grateful for it. My deep appreciation goes to the many people who have fostered this book in one way or another.

I thank the late Eugene and Nane Bernard for bringing France to my doorstep, and with it, a whole new understanding of food and how it connects people to each other. To my friends Bruce and Blanche Rubin, Kathy Nilsson, Nancy Barcelo, Sandra Fairbank, and Fiona Hamersley: Thank you for your encouragement, enthusiasm, and friendship throughout this process. To Cindy Anderson: Special thanks for reading the manuscript from cover to cover as if it were a novel, and one without a plot at that. Such an act of friendship never can be sufficiently rewarded. Fellow jam-maker Bonnie Shershow willingly carried on exhaustive conversations about fruit in jars. To Kristin Wainwright: Thank you for your practical advice. To Michael Melford: Thanks for your legal advice. Thanks also to Andrea Chesman for skillful and diligent editing.

I would like to acknowledge those whose recipes found their way into this book: Elisabeth Calder Childs for Blueberry-Raspberry Jam; Eugene Bernard for Plums in Plum Liqueur, Framboise, Marzipan-Stuffed Dates and Prunes, the Fruit Jellies, and Mystery Truffles; my brother-in-law, Fidel Luevano, for Chile de Árbol Salsa; and Linda Kucera for Triple-Chocolate Walnut Cookies.

Finally, Frank Vargas gets the Most Supportive Husband award. This book simply would not have happened without him. My son Luke is the very best one-boy cheering section any mother could ask for. Thanks, guys. You're the best.

Preface

IN THE 1970S, I started a restaurant with a group of friends in a rural upstate New York town. As fate would have it, our nearest neighbor was an amiable Frenchman, newly retired from his position as executive chef at a prestigious Manhattan restaurant. Eugene Bernard, known to friends and family simply as Bernard, had an excess of energy and time on his hands and made frequent appearances at our back door. With a fierce set of standards and a healthy dose of humor, he helped us transform our six-table vegetarian roadside café into a large and charming country restaurant.

Bernard's wife, Nane, gave us packages of chocolate truffles every Christmas. Although Nane and Bernard are gone now, I cannot bite into a dense and chocolatey truffle without suddenly hearing Nane's voice, her broken English lapsing into French in a moment of pique. I can see her rabbit hutches behind the garden where the giant parsley plants she tended thrived. And I can picture Bernard, standing in the restaurant kitchen, nearly knocking me over with friendly bear slaps on the back, his whole being shaking with laughter at my earnest beginner's attempt to make coulibiac from a Time-Life cookbook. "My friends," he would say, shaking his head, "why you want to make sopheesticated cooking in the country?" All these thoughts come flooding back in one bite, in one quick taste of bitter cocoa against a thick mouthful of sweet chocolate.

So many of our fondest memories revolve around food, memories that above all are connected to people. When I make Nane's truffles to give to a friend, I'm adding another link to a chain, passing on the love I have for her in my little package. Gifts of food can carry on cherished traditions and help us to create new memories.

I was too relieved to look back when I closed the door on a restaurant career. No more fourteen-hour days, no more coolers full of perishable ingredients, no more temperamental dishwashers and no-show plumbers. I had a suitcase full of memories, however. The Bernards, once simply neighbors, had become an important part of my personal history as mentors and close friends. I had no regrets.

Without a restaurant, though, I had to tame my grand-scale truffle-making urges. Now I time them to coincide with holidays. In the late summer I make framboise and jam for my own pleasure and give them to family and friends for theirs.

More than ever, our lives seem hurried and full of meals spooned from take-out boxes. Making special treats for others is a lovely way to slow down. Our grandmothers were connected to their bodies when they kneaded dough, connected to the rhythms of the seasons when they made preserves, connected to their communities when they brought soup to a sick friend. We have severed these natural connections in the rush of modern life, and now we must make an effort to restore them. We need them, and so do our friends.

chapter one

The Art of Giving

Sharing food is a primal human experience. Rituals like the communal breaking of bread, the passing of a cup of wine, or the offering of a special treat to our ancestors at the cemetery on All Souls' Day bear witness to how deeply this sharing is embedded in our collective psyche. In an age of cyberspace, E-mail, and instant everything, the act of giving and receiving reminds us of these roots. To prepare a gift of food, we must take time, one of our most precious commodities, away from our everyday routines and obligations. In giving that time, we are expressing something very personal: that we care, that our friends matter, that it is important to sustain our relationships.

A gift of food is nourishment on many levels, for the giver as well as for the receiver. Without a doubt, the recipient of a homemade gift must feel nurtured. Perhaps we are comforting a friend. Our gift of chocolate and a permission slip to put on the pj's, crawl into bed, and turn on a favorite junky TV show may be just what the doctor ordered. Our great aunts may be surprised and delighted to open a tin of their favorite cookies that they no longer bake themselves. And imagine the pleasure on the face of a child's teacher to discover in her package some soothing herb tea, a batch of shortbread, and a book by her favorite author. The opportunities for giving homemade gifts of food await us in every season and for every reason.

Luckily, you need no special training to create fabulous food gifts. In these pages you will find ideas and recipes for all levels of cooks, from the culinarily challenged to the experienced. Framboise, for instance, is the absolute cornerstone of my own personal cottage industry. Add raspberries to vodka and let soak for 2 months. Stir in sugar. Taste. Pour into a clean wine bottle and tie with a beautiful ribbon. Presto! A lovely ruby red testament to the last days of summer. If you can read and if you can measure, you can give a friend a gift of food.

wrapping your GIFT OF FOOD

When you have worked hard to prepare something truly delicious to give to a friend, it deserves a little extra attention and care in the presentation. The contents of the jar may taste fabulous, but the incentive to open the jar and have a lick must be there, too. A beautiful package is an invitation, a promise of what waits beneath the wrapping. Each chapter contains some wrapping suggestions in its introduction. In addition, this chapter contains some general presentation ideas and a few gift-wrapping projects.

give yourself the GIFT OF ORGANIZATION

It's all in the planning. How much time you have and how many gifts you want to make will determine your choice of gift. If you are making a lot of holiday gifts, choose something that can be made ahead, like jam, or made quickly, like muffin mix. For special occasions when you will make only one or two gifts, you may want to take more time, perhaps fashioning a keepsake box or putting together a gift basket. Whatever you decide, give some thought to how you will wrap your gift before you even start making it, collect the necessary materials, and set aside time for each step.

Collect wrapping materials ahead of time, to avoid feeling rushed at the last minute. And while you're out shopping, buy yourself a plastic box to keep scissors, tape, ribbons, tags, labels, raffia, metallic and colored pens, rubber stamps, and other materials in one place, and store it in a closet. Or designate a drawer in your house for keeping wrapping supplies handy. Then even if you haven't planned everything down to the last detail, you can still create a spur-of-the-moment gift with relative ease.

what's your **STYLE?**

Before you shop, think in terms of a theme or color scheme that will help you focus when designing your gift wrap. Are you a nature lover who prefers simple, earthy wraps? Consider using brown paper, string, raffia, handmade paper flecked with flower petals, and leaf-shaped tags for your gift. Or do you like glamour and a bit of sparkle? Choose gold and silver ribbons and paper, metallic tissue, cellophane, or shiny ribbons, or glue some pearls or faux jewels to your gift tag. Do you love ethereal-looking gifts with pale wrappings and gauzy ribbons? This is a chance to have fun and express yourself. Next time you are in an upscale coffee bar or gourmet food store, look around at the wrappings and notice what the people who do this for a living have dreamed up. Or take your inspiration from a magazine or a stroll through an art supply store.

what's your **BUDGET?**

You don't have to break the bank to create a beautiful gift. Cellophane bags and pretty wrapping paper can make your gift elegant without putting you in the red. You have already saved some money by making the gift yourself instead of buying it. Now splurge a little on a sheet of handmade paper for your jam jars—one will cover many—or buy some fancy ribbon from the fabric store. If you're feeling expansive, here's a chance to buy a special friend that charlotte mold she's been yearning for and fill it with cookies.

WRAPPING: the basic ingredients

Baskets, paper, fabric, and gift tags or labels are the basic ingredients for wrapping food gifts. Ribbons and ornaments add extra flair to the packaging.

WHERE TO LOOK FOR WRAPPING SUPPLIES

Wrapping supplies are everywhere. When you are out shopping, stock up on them so you have them on hand—just as you stock up on butter, flour, and eggs from the grocery store.

SUPERMARKETS: Plain coffee bags, canning jars, disposable loaf pans, parchment paper, paraffin, muffin-cup liners.

HARDWARE AND COOKWARE SHOPS: Canning jars, jam-making supplies, French preserving jars with metal rims (look for Luminarc brand), cookie tins, canisters, jam labels, glass bottles and corks, honey jars, baskets, gift bags.

STATIONERY, ART SUPPLY, AND CRAFT STORES: Labels, tags, handmade paper, rubber stamps, ribbon, raffia, stickers, metallic pens, craft boxes, cellophane bags, baskets, gift bags.

FABRIC STORES: Fabric for jam jars, fancy ribbon, millinery trinkets to decorate packages.

(continued on page 4)

CELLOPHANE

Like punch at a party, a gift wrapped in cellophane has a little extra sparkle. It is also quick, easy, and inexpensive. Most stores that sell gift wrap and party favors also carry clear or patterned cellophane bags. Your cookies, candies, pecans, and even a stack of small jam jars fit nicely in a cellophane bag. Add a beautiful wide ribbon and you're in business. Use cellophane from a roll to package loaf cakes, gift baskets, and large gift containers like baking dishes or molds, following the directions on page 5 on how to wrap large baskets.

CONTAINERS

Think beyond baskets and cellophane bags and keep your eyes peeled at tag sales and second-hand stores for pretty one-of-a-kind plates, bowls, ice cream molds, and vintage napkins and tea towels. Beautiful gift bags from a stationery store solve the container problem easily. They come in all sizes and shapes. And don't forget about using cookware as a gift that does double-duty as a container. Your tea cake could be wrapped and placed in a new loaf pan and your cookies could be assembled and wrapped in a new baking dish. Consider the recipient's taste and needs when deciding how to wrap your gift.

PAPER

Beautiful, sturdy wrapping paper will go a long way toward embellishing your gift, but think about widening your horizons. Handmade paper or special single sheets of beautiful paper, parchment paper, glassine paper, metallic paper, brown craft paper, or even foreign-language newspapers make unusual gift wraps.

FABRICS

Don't limit yourself to paper. Fabrics also make interesting wraps. A loaf cake wrapped in cellophane and then in a pretty tea towel makes two gifts in one. Or make a simple pouch for your gift with your favorite vintage fabric, a pretty cloth napkin, a square of colored organdy overlaid with a white square, or a lace handkerchief.

GIFT TAGS AND LABELS

Stationery and office supply stores offer a wide range of options for gift tags. Oak tag and metal rim tags are easy to find, as are file labels with red or blue borders. Look for special jam labels at cookware shops, or design your own label and take it to the copy center to duplicate on adhesive paper.

RIBBON

When choosing ribbon, think luxury. Silk, satin, organdy, gauze, velvet, or wide wire-edged ribbon; metallic cording; and star-studded metallic wire are the finishing touches that elevate your gift from the ordinary to the extraordinary. For a natural look, choose grosgrain or linen ribbons in muted earth tones, straw-colored raffia, and cotton string or twine.

ORNAMENTS

Like special ribbon, an ornament attached to your box of candy or jar of jam will distinguish your gift. Look in fabric, craft, or second-hand stores for tassels, millinery accessories, small toys or Christmas ornaments, dried flowers, vintage beads, buttons, crystal chandelier remnants, and pearls. From the world around you, choose nuts, acorns, small pine cones, or evergreen sprigs. They can be spray painted or not, and attached to your package or gift tag with glue or ribbon.

HOW TO WRAP a large gift basket

▶ *What you need:*
   Measuring tape, scissors, roll of cellophane, twist tie, at least 1 yard of wide ribbon, clear packing tape.

1. Open the measuring tape to about 5 feet. Center the basket on the tape. (If the basket is not square, measure the longest side.) Bring the tape up to the center of the basket handle and pinch the two sides of the tape together. Measure 8 to 12 inches above the handle, adjusting the tape as necessary.

SPECIAL OCCASION GIFT BASKETS

Baskets offer endless possibilities for gift combinations. You needn't make every item in the basket yourself. With some store-bought tea, local honey, cloth napkins, two egg cups, a jam pot, and a silver spoon or two from a tag sale, you can build a whole basket around just one jar of your homemade jam.

If the basket is deep, fill it with crumpled tissue paper or colored shredded paper from a craft store. Arrange your gifts on top to show them off to their best effect and wrap the whole basket in cellophane (see below left) For your friend, opening a basket full of individually wrapped gifts is like finding her own secret treasure chest.

A BASKET FOR TEATIME

Ginger Pennies (page 118)

Palets de Dames (page 112)

Lavender-Lemon Tea Cakes (page 96)

Chai Mix (page 26)

Darjeeling tea

Chamomile tea

A tea cozy

A cellophane bag of brown sugar cubes

A jar of special honey

(continued on page 6)

2. Using the above measurement, cut 2 lengths of cellophane. Place 1 length on the work surface and center the second length over it in the opposite direction to form a cross. Center your filled basket on the cellophane.

3. Draw the two sides of 1 length of cellophane up to the center of the basket handle, gather them, and secure them with a twist tie. Repeat with the second length of cellophane and secure it with another twist tie. Tie a knot with the ribbon and remove the twist ties. Make a bow.

4. Adjust the cellophane on the bottom of the basket by folding the gaps and pulling them taut underneath the basket. Secure the cellophane with clear packing tape on the underside of the basket.

gift TAGS

While you can purchase gift tags from a stationery or office supply store, it's fun to make your own. A handmade gift tag can transform even the simplest wrapping into something special. Children and adults of all ages enjoy making these.

▶ *What you need:*

Pencil; assorted colored, white, and printed sturdy papers; thin ribbon or raffia; metallic and colored pens; scissors or pinking shears; paper punch; glue; old holiday cards; buttons, baubles, and beads.

fruit and vegetable cards: Draw or trace the shapes of fruits, vegetables, or leaves that correspond to the contents of your gift (lemons, apples, oranges, peppers, eggplants) on brightly colored paper. Cut out each shape, punch a hole at the corner, thread it with fine ribbon, and write a message or title on the card.

holiday cards: Draw or trace (using cookie cutters) stars, bells, holly leaves, Christmas trees, mittens, or Christmas tree ornaments out of plain and patterned or shiny paper. Cut out both shapes and glue the papers together. Punch a hole at the corner, thread with fine ribbon, and write your message on the plain side.

recycled card tags: Cut out images from old holiday cards. Cut circles or squares out of sturdy white paper with pinking shears, and glue the images onto the cards. Punch a hole in each card and thread it with fine ribbon. Write your message or title on the back of the card.

affix-it cards: Cut out squares of heavy colored or white paper, or use tags from the office supply store. Glue on buttons, pearls, faux jewels, glitter, holly leaves, kids' stickers, or whatever strikes your fancy. Punch a hole at the corner of each card and thread with fine ribbon. Write a message on the card.

FLOWERPOT family fun

Flowerpots decorated by your child make excellent containers for a teacher's gift of candy or cookies. Be sure to line the interior of the pot with tissue or cellophane, add your gift, and enclose the filled flowerpot in a cellophane bag. If you decorate a large pot, wrap it in a sheet of cellophane or tissue, gather the edges at the top, and tie with a ribbon.

Kinderpot

▶ *What you need:*

New small or large clay flowerpot; poster paints; paintbrushes; optional items include white shellac or clear acrylic varnish from a craft store and a paintbrush.

1. Wash the flowerpot and leave to dry thoroughly.

2. Paint a design with poster paint and allow to dry.

3. If you like, apply a finishing coat of shellac or clear acrylic varnish.

Gold or Silver Pot

▶ *What you need:*

New small or large clay flowerpot; bay leaves or other small, sturdy leaves; Scotch tape; gold or silver spray paint; cardboard box.

1. Wash the flowerpot and leave to dry thoroughly.

2. Using loops of Scotch tape, attach leaves to the pot in a decorative pattern. (The tape should not be visible.)

3. Place the pot upside down in a large cardboard box outside or in a well-ventilated area indoors. Spray with the metallic paint and leave to dry. When dry, remove the leaves and tape.

snappy **JAR WRAPPING**

Jars of jam or preserved fruits can be simply wrapped in brightly colored tissue paper. Set the jar on a doubled square of tissue, gather it at the top, and tie with a ribbon. Voilà!

For only slightly more effort, you can make a cover for the top of the jar. It shows off the contents and the recipient can be cheered by a prettily wrapped jar in the cupboard. Paper or fabric, the choice is yours. If you come across wrapping paper with strawberries on it, by all means use it for your strawberry jam, or go the natural route with brown-paper covers tied with string. (See Wrapping: The Basic Ingredients, page 3, for more suggestions.)

Jar Covers for Half-Pint Canning Jars

▶ *What you need:*

Heavy wrapping paper, craft paper, or fabric; scissors or pinking shears; Scotch tape; a rubber band; ribbon; raffia or string.

1. For each jar top, cut a 6-inch square or circle from paper or fabric. If using fabric, cut with pinking shears. (For wide-mouthed pint and quart jars, cut paper or fabric in 7-inch squares. If your jar doesn't conform to any of these specifications, cut a square out of scrap paper first to determine the size cover you want to make.)

2. Make a small loop with a piece of Scotch tape and affix it to the jar top. This is to hold slippery paper or fabric in place while you tie on the ribbon.

3. Center the fabric over the jar top, pull it down, and secure it under the jar band with a rubber band.

4. Cut a 24-inch length of ribbon or string and tie it firmly around the jar. If using raffia, cut 2 lengths to make a double thickness. If the ribbon covers the rubber band, you can leave it in place. Or simply remove the rubber band when the cover is secured with the ribbon.

simple fabric **GIFT POUCHES**

Squares of vintage fabric, pretty cloth napkins, luxurious velvet or upholstery remnants, even lace handkerchiefs provide easy, unusual alternatives to paper gift wraps. Cookies and candies in cellophane bags, small tube cakes wrapped in cellophane, and jars of jam and preserved fruits are all candidates for this wrapping treatment.

▶ *What you need:*

Scissors, heavy card stock, pinking shears, fabric, ribbon.

1. Cut a square of card stock to a size that will accommodate the bottom of your gift.

2. With pinking shears, cut a square or circle of fabric with a diameter of 5 or 6 times the width of the cardboard square.

3. Place your gift on the cardboard square and center it on the fabric.

4. Draw the fabric to the top of the gift, arranging it in pleats, and tie it firmly in place with ribbon.

a pretty **PAPER CONE**

What child would not be delighted to wake up on Christmas morning and find a cone full of treats hanging on the tree? These cones, from a Victorian tradition, can be carried to a friend's house, too. They make sweet little baskets for cookies and candies. Use heavy wrapping paper, foil wrapping paper, or create something more delicate by gluing fine paper to a backing of sturdy white or colored paper. Put your treats in a cellophane bag first to keep them fresh.

▶ *What you need:*

> 9 by 12-inch piece of construction paper, pencil, ruler, scissors, fancy wrapping paper, glue stick or double-sided Scotch tape, paper punch, ¹/₄- to ¹/₂-inch-wide satin ribbon, paper doily (optional).

1. Fold a 9 by 12-inch piece of construction paper in half lengthwise. Position the folded paper vertical to you, with the unfolded edge on the left. Make a pencil mark on the unfolded edge 3 inches from the top of the paper.

2. Draw a line from the bottom, folded right-hand corner to the mark and cut along the line.

3. With the paper still folded, cut a half arc, starting at the mark and going to the top of the fold. When you unfold the paper, you should end up with an ice-cream-cone shape, rounded at the top.

4. Place the pattern on some pretty wrapping paper (you can cut several at a time) and cut along the lines.

5. Use a glue stick to make a line along one straight edge of the flat cone, or affix a strip of double-sided tape. Roll the opposite edge of the paper toward the sticky edge and press the seam to close.

6. Punch two holes opposite each other at the top of the cone and thread ribbon through them to make a handle. Attach the ribbon to the inside of the cone with the Scotch tape. Tuck a doily inside the cone if you like, and fill the cone with cookies or candy.

NOTE: If the paper is delicate, glue it along the edges to a backing of heavier plain paper before rolling it into a cone.

TOPPING OFF a bottle

You can give your bottles of homemade liqueur or vinegar a custom look by dipping the tops in colored wax. Choose a color that corresponds to the contents of the bottle: a soft green for vinegar, a dark purple for blackberry wine, a cheery pink for framboise.

Look for paraffin (wax) in the canning section of the supermarket or at the hardware store.

▶ *What you need:*

A block of paraffin; a clean, dry tin can; a small saucepan; a plastic spoon; colored crayons; some newspaper; a pretty adhesive label; raffia or ribbon.

1. Break off a chunk from a block of paraffin about the size of a golf ball. Place it in a clean, dry tin can. Place the can in a pan of water. Bring the water to a boil and turn off the heat.

2. Add a colored crayon to the can and stir with a plastic spoon until the wax is melted. Wax is extremely flammable, so exercise caution. Do not attempt to microwave this!

3. Spread a piece of newspaper on your work surface, remove the can from the hot water, and place it on the paper. Test the color by spooning some wax onto the newspaper, and adjust by adding more crayon if necessary.

4. Immerse the top of the firmly corked bottle so that wax covers the first 2 inches, remove it, and allow to cool for a few seconds. Dip it several times, always allowing it to cool between the coatings, until you can no longer see the cork through the wax. Let the wax set until firm.

5. Wipe the bottle clean and affix the label. Finish off with a ribbon or a piece of raffia wrapped several times around the neck of the bottle.

a keepsake **CANDY BOX**

Although this candy box is not difficult to make, it will take planning and $1^1/_2$ to 2 hours to complete. To assemble everything you need in one trip, your best bet is to visit an art supply store that carries bookbinding supplies. You should be able to find beautiful papers there, as well as glue and a bone folder. A bone folder is a bookbinding tool used for smoothing paper.

Think of the recipient when you are choosing paper. What are her favorite colors? Does he love all things Japanese? Or does elegant marbleized paper fit the bill? Your friend will think of you every time she reaches for a pair of earrings from the lovely box, or perhaps he will keep the box on his desk for storing small odds and ends.

▶ *What you need:*

5-inch cardboard cylindrical craft box, 2 sheets (about 20 by 30 inches each) of contrasting paper, tape measure, pencil, scissors, compass, ruler, bone folder, waxed paper, methyl cellulose adhesive or 50/50 mixture of methyl cellulose and PVA (polyvinyl acetate) adhesive, $^1/_2$-inch paintbrush for applying glue.

Box Bottom

1. Measure the circumference of the box and add 1 inch. Measure the height of the box and add 1 inch. Cut a strip of paper for the outside of the box according to the above measurements.

2. Measure $^1/_2$ inch from each long edge of the paper and mark with pencil on the wrong side. Draw a line and then fold the paper to the inside along the line. Hold it up to the box to check the fit before gluing. With scissors, snip the paper from the outside edge to the fold on both sides at $^3/_4$-inch intervals.

3. Stack 2 long pieces of waxed paper on top of each other on the work surface. This is your gluing surface. Lay the paper, wrong side up, on top of the waxed paper. Apply the glue to the paper, starting in the middle and brushing out and over the edge onto the waxed paper.

4. Pick up the paper, remove the first gluing surface, and set the paper on the second, clean piece of waxed paper. Turn the box on its side and press it to the paper by rolling it along the lines. Carefully press the flaps onto the bottom and inside of the box. Smooth with a bone folder to remove wrinkles and air bubbles.

5. Measure and cut a strip for the inside of the box using contrasting paper. It should be 1 inch longer than the circumference and $^1/_2$ inch wider than the height. Draw a line $^1/_2$ inch from the long edge on the wrong side of the paper, and fold the paper along the line. With scissors, snip the paper as before from the outside edge to the fold at $^3/_4$-inch intervals. This time you will have only one fold. Hold it up to the box to check the fit before gluing.

6. Apply glue to the inside of the box, covering the side and a rim of about $^1/_2$ inch at the bottom edge. Affix the paper to the inside of the box, aligning the even edge with the top of the box and the snipped edge with the bottom edge of the box. Smooth with the bone folder to remove wrinkles and air bubbles.

7. Draw and then cut a circle of the same paper used in step 6 to fit on the inside bottom of the box. Place it in the box to check the fit before gluing. Lay the circle on a piece of clean waxed paper with the wrong side up and apply glue, starting in the middle and brushing out and over the edge onto the waxed paper. Glue the paper to the inside bottom of the box. Smooth with the bone folder to remove wrinkles and air bubbles.

8. Repeat step 6 for the outside bottom of the box, using the same paper as you did for the outside of the box.

Box Top

1. Repeat steps 1 through 8, this time covering the top of the box in step 8.

2. Allow the box to dry overnight before lining with tissue and waxed paper and filling with your homemade candies.

SENDING GIFTS in the mail

Making a gift, wrapping it, and *then* wrapping it for sending in the mail (not to mention getting it to the post office or UPS in good time) automatically qualify you for a place in line for sainthood. A few simple steps help ensure that your gift will arrive safely.

First, choose something that can take a little tough handling. Jams that have been preserved in a water bath and are thus tightly sealed, for instance, travel well. Sturdy cookies, packed in a tin with a layer of crumpled waxed paper to keep them from jiggling around, also travel without incident. A bottle that could leak or a gift that needs refrigeration obviously is not a candidate. Use your common sense.

After you have wrapped your gift, wrap it again in bubble wrap and pack it in a box with plenty of crumpled paper to keep it secure. Finally, wrap *that* box snugly in another, larger box, using Styrofoam peanuts (recycled) or crumpled newsprint to keep it in place. You can save some mess and fuss for the recipient by making two "pillows" of Styrofoam peanuts. Enclose them in large plastic bags and arrange them under, around, and over your gift.

Put the sender's name and address and your name and address on a card inside the box before sealing with packing tape and addressing the outside of the box.

breakfast foods

chapter two

The Gift of Time

A mother on a tight schedule, a student away at college, and a busy weekend hostess are just a few of the candidates who will appreciate a gift of homemade granola or hot-chocolate mix. Breakfast foods, when we have the time to enjoy them, are comforting, even reassuring. They have somehow managed to hold their own against fashionable food trends. A hot cup of tea and an old-fashioned corn muffin on a chilly morning continue to cheer us and remind us of the perfection of simple things.

Most of the recipes in this chapter are simple measure-and-mix ones that can be assembled quickly and easily. I love to use 1-pound coffee bags from the supermarket (they hold about 4 cups) for mixes, but they're good for granola, too. You can usually convince someone at the deli counter or a store manager to let you buy the white or brown bags at a modest price. Affix a pretty label to the bag and write mix instructions by hand on the back, or punch a hole in the top of the bag and attach a card with a loop of ribbon. You can involve the kids and let them decorate the bag with rubber stamps, too.

Pretty quart-sized canisters, large glass-top canning jars from a flea market or yard sale, or simple cellophane bags tied with pretty ribbons all make good containers for granola. Breakfast baskets are a cinch: pancake mix with blueberry sauce and a jar of pure maple syrup, muffin mix and a jar of your special homemade jam, a box of tea, and your hot-chocolate mix or one from the gourmet food store all add up to a welcome package.

out-of-this-world FIVE-GRAIN PANCAKE and WAFFLE MIX

5 cups unbleached all-purpose flour

2¹⁄₂ cups whole-wheat flour

1 cup rye flour

1 cup corn flour

1 cup brown or white rice flour

1 cup yellow cornmeal

1 cup powdered buttermilk

³⁄₄ cup firmly packed dark brown sugar or Sucanat (granulated dried cane juice)

¹⁄₄ cup baking powder

2 tablespoons salt

4 teaspoons baking soda

1 cup toasted wheat germ

1 cup oat bran

▶ MAKES FIVE 3-CUP PACKAGES

Finding all of these ingredients is not as difficult as it might seem at first glance. One trip to a natural food store ought to do the trick. If you're stumped, simply substitute more white or whole-wheat flour for the missing exotic grain. The rice flour is essential for crisp waffles, so if you can't find it, just call it pancake mix.

The name for these pancakes was inspired by a set of rubber stamps my son had: The blue-and-gold planets and stars we stamped on the white coffee bag we used for packing the mix just seemed to fit. And, as it turns out, the pancakes really are out of this world. Don't forget to include the directions for whipping up a batch.

MEASURE all of the ingredients except the wheat germ and oat bran into a large bowl and mix thoroughly with your hands. Sift the flour mixture and add the wheat germ and oat bran. Mix again.

DIVIDE in 5 portions of 3 cups each. If you want to make larger packages, simply distribute the mix in amounts that are divisible by 1¹⁄₂ cups.

1 egg for pancakes or 2 eggs for waffles

1 to 1¹⁄₂ cups milk

2 tablespoons melted butter

1 teaspoon vanilla extract (optional)

1¹⁄₂ cups mix

▶ DIRECTIONS FOR MAKING TEN TO TWELVE 4-INCH PANCAKES OR FOUR OR FIVE WAFFLES

IN A BOWL, beat together the egg(s), 1 cup milk, melted butter, and vanilla. Stir in the mix. Thin with additional milk if needed. Cook on a lightly oiled griddle or waffle iron until browned on both sides.

Buttermilk Pancakes   For 10 to 12 pancakes

1 1/2 cups mix
1 egg
1 to 1 1/2 cups milk
2 tablespoons melted butter
1 teaspoon vanilla (opt.)

Beat egg or eggs with milk, melted butter
vanilla. Add mix.

Holly
and
Matthew

orange BUCKWHEAT PANCAKE and WAFFLE MIX

4 cups buckwheat flour

3¹/₂ cups whole-wheat flour

2¹/₂ cups unbleached all-purpose flour

1 cup firmly packed dark brown sugar

1 tablespoon baking powder

1 tablespoon salt

1 tablespoon plus 2 teaspoons baking soda

1 tablespoon granulated dried orange peel

2 eggs, separated

¹/₂ cup plain yogurt

³/₄ cup orange juice

3 tablespoons butter, melted

1¹/₂ cups mix

2 to 3 tablespoons milk (optional)

▶ MAKES FOUR 3-CUP PACKAGES

Buckwheat pancakes are an old-fashioned treat, a nice gift for a weekend hostess in the city or country. You could bring along a jar of pure maple syrup, or mix up a batch of orange-flavored honey butter: Heat a scant ¹/₂ cup honey with a few tablespoons of unsalted butter (the amount determined by your preference) and some finely grated orange zest. Pour it into a heatproof half-pint jar, then label with instructions to reheat by setting the jar in a pan of hot water and to store in the refrigerator.

MEASURE all the ingredients except the orange peel into a large bowl and mix thoroughly with your hands. Sift and add the orange peel. Mix again.

DIVIDE into 4 portions of 3 cups each.

▶ DIRECTIONS FOR MAKING TEN TO TWELVE 4-INCH PANCAKES OR FIVE OR SIX WAFFLES

IN A BOWL, beat together the egg yolks, yogurt, orange juice, and melted butter. Stir in the mix. Beat the egg whites until they form soft peaks, then fold them into the batter. Buckwheat flour makes a thick batter, which is perfect for waffles. Add a few more tablespoons of milk for a thinner pancake batter. Cook on a lightly oiled griddle or waffle iron until browned on both sides.

new england CORN-MUFFIN MIX

▶ MAKES FOUR 3-CUP GIFT PACKAGES

I bet your mother wishes she had a few of these packages in her pantry when you were a kid. You can make a busy mom happy with this practical mix, which is so much yummier than its store-bought counterpart. The muffins are New England style, a little on the sweet side. The package directions make 6 muffins, good for whipping up for breakfast or supper for a small family—no leftovers to freeze. Expand the gift with a jar of your favorite jam, a muffin tin, or a package of muffin-cup liners.

2 cups yellow cornmeal

9 cups unbleached all-purpose flour

1³/₄ cups sugar

2 tablespoons plus 1 teaspoon baking powder

4 teaspoons baking soda

2 teaspoons salt

MEASURE all the ingredients together in a large bowl and mix thoroughly with your hands. Sift and mix again.

DIVIDE into 4 portions of 3 cups each. If you want to make larger packages, simply distribute the mix in amounts that are divisible by 1¹/₂ cups.

▶ DIRECTIONS FOR MAKING 6 MUFFINS

1 egg

¹/₂ cup plus 1 tablespoon milk

¹/₄ cup (¹/₂ stick) unsalted butter, melted

1¹/₂ cups mix

PREHEAT the oven to 425°. Grease 6 muffin cups or line with paper liners.

IN A BOWL, whisk together the egg, milk, and melted butter and stir in the mix. Divide among the prepared muffin cups. Reduce the oven temperature to 400° and bake for 15 to 18 minutes, until golden brown and springy on top.

BAKING GRANOLA

The best pans for toasting granola are heavy baking sheets with 1-inch rims (sometimes called jelly-roll pans), as they keep the cereal from spilling. Line them with aluminum foil to keep the mess (and cleanup) at a minimum, and the foil can be reused for your next batch.

PERSONALIZING GRANOLA

You can invent your own granola recipe by adapting this one. For example, add toasted coconut or your favorite nuts, substitute chopped dried fruit or raisins for the cranberries, or use honey or molasses instead of maple syrup. Puffed cereals like puffed rice, corn, or millet contribute another interesting texture. Follow this recipe for your first batch or two and then experiment with new ingredients, keeping in mind the ideal proportions: For 16 cups of granola, at least 11 cups should be flakes, and 6 cups of the flakes should be rolled oats.

maple-cranberry **GRANOLA**

▶ MAKES FOUR 4-CUP PACKAGES

Early risers, late-night snackers—who wouldn't like a gift of this homemade fresher-than-fresh cereal? Pack it in a pretty canister or a cellophane bag tied with a ribbon, and add a bag of your favorite gourmet coffee to the gift.

Don't be discouraged if you can't find all the grains in the recipe at your local natural food store. Granola formulas are very forgiving, so just use what you can find.

8 cups old-fashioned rolled oats	$^2/_3$ cup mild vegetable oil
$1^1/_2$ cups barley flakes	$1^1/_3$ cups pure maple syrup
$1^1/_2$ cups wheat flakes	2 tablespoons vanilla extract
2 cups puffed corn cereal	2 teaspoons salt
2 cups sliced almonds	1 cup dried cranberries

PREHEAT the oven to 350°. Line 2 large baking sheets with aluminum foil.

IN A LARGE BOWL, combine the oats, barley flakes, wheat flakes, puffed corn, and almonds. In a saucepan, combine the oil, maple syrup, vanilla, and salt and heat to a simmer. Pour the warmed oil mixture over the grains and mix well to coat.

DIVIDE the granola evenly between the prepared baking sheets. Bake for 20 minutes. Remove the baking sheets from the oven and stir the granola. Return the baking sheets to the oven but switch their positions so that the sheet that had been on the top rack is now on the bottom rack. This will help the granola to brown evenly. Continue to bake, removing the pans, stirring the granola, and rotating the pans every 5 to 7 minutes for about 15 more minutes. The granola browns quickly near the end of toasting, so check it often to keep it from scorching. When the granola is a deep golden brown, remove it from the oven and let it rest until cool.

POUR into a big bowl and mix with the cranberries. Store in an airtight tin for up to 2 weeks for maximum freshness.

mexican-style **HOT-CHOCOLATE MIX**

▶ MAKES 1 CUP MIX, ENOUGH FOR 16 SERVINGS

Mexican chocolate adds a nice touch to a gift basket of breakfast foods. But finding a Mexican brand such as Abuelita or Ibarra can be a problem if you don't live near a Latin grocery store. A pretty 8-ounce jar tied with a brown satin ribbon makes a nice presentation for this mix, and you can also give it to your favorite chocoholic with a selection of other chocolate goodies. The recipe multiplies nicely by as much as four for larger-scale production, and the mix will keep for about 6 months.

$1/2$ cup sugar

2 tablespoons whole almonds

1 ounce bittersweet or semisweet chocolate, coarsely chopped

$1/4$ cup Dutch-process cocoa powder

1 teaspoon vanilla extract

1 teaspoon ground cinnamon

$1/2$ teaspoon ground cloves

COMBINE the sugar and almonds in a food processor and process until the almonds are finely ground. Add the chocolate, cocoa, vanilla, cinnamon, and cloves and process again until the mixture is finely ground. Store in an airtight container.

▶ DIRECTIONS FOR MAKING 1 CUP HOT CHOCOLATE

HEAT 1 cup milk with 1 tablespoon mix and whisk until frothy.

CHAI mix

► MAKES ³/₄ CUP, ENOUGH FOR 24 SERVINGS

This sweet and spicy Indian tea is my own personal comfort drink. It makes a wonderful midmorning pick-me-up and an effective antidote to drowsiness in the afternoon. Tie it up with a ribbon in a cellophane bag and give it to a friend with a package of good Assam tea and a bag of your favorite dainty cookies. Or add a volume of Rumi's poetry for a dreamy mini retreat.

The following formula is only a suggestion. Mixing the spices is something like blending a perfume. Here, ginger and pepper notes balance the heady cardamom and clove, but you could play around with combinations that suit your own preferences. Other ingredients worth considering are dried orange peel, fennel, nutmeg, mace, juniper, and rose petals. The recipe can be multiplied by four or more for larger-scale production, and the mix will stay lively for about 6 months if contained in a tightly closed jar or tin.

5 tablespoons cardamom pods

2 tablespoons whole cloves

1 tablespoon coriander seeds

8 2-inch-long sticks cinnamon, broken into pieces

¹/₄ teaspoon black peppercorns

2 whole star anise

1 teaspoon ground ginger

COMBINE all of the ingredients except the ginger in a ungreased heavy skillet. Stir over medium heat for 2 to 3 minutes, or until fragrant, to toast the spices.

ADD the ginger and spoon the mixture into a mortar in manageable batches. Pound briefly, just enough to crush the spices coarsely. (You could also break them up with a rolling pin or pulse them briefly in a spice grinder.) Transfer to an airtight container for storage.

► DIRECTIONS FOR MAKING
   CHAI FOR TWO

IN A SMALL SAUCEPAN, combine 1 cup milk with 2 rounded teaspoons Chai Mix and 2 teaspoons brown sugar, or to taste. Heat just until the mixture bubbles at the edges. Turn off the heat and cover the pot with a lid. Let steep for about 10 minutes while you make the tea.

BREW a pot of Assam or Darjeeling tea using 2 cups boiling water and 2 teaspoons tea. Reheat the spiced milk if necessary and strain it into 2 large teacups. Pour in the hot tea and enjoy.

jams and marmalades

chapter three

Tastes of Summer

If you've never experienced the satisfaction of making a batch of jam, beware: It can become an obsession. On the plus side, your friends will benefit from your new fixation, and your holiday shopping will be complete by the end of the summer. With a few jars of your own special brand of jam in the cupboard, you'll always be ready with a gift for your host or hostess, your child's teacher, or a neighbor who needs cheering up. And since the jam is ready and waiting, you also may be inspired to make a loaf of bread or stir up a batch of corn-muffin mix (page 23) to go with it.

Buying beautiful organic fruit in season from a farm stand or picking your own is one of the pleasures of making jam. More and more farm trucks are finding their way to urban farmers' markets, so city dwellers can also participate in what was once a country pursuit. Any fruit that is used for preserving must be in tip-top condition. You cannot rescue slightly overripe or bruised fruits by putting them into a preserving jar.

While it's preferable to use freshly picked produce, if you'd rather be at the beach than home making jam, then freeze the fruit and make the jam later. The fruit you've carefully selected will be superior to a commercially frozen product.

Freeze peaches, apricots, and plums whole in heavy-duty plastic bags. Wipe the fruit with a damp cloth first if they need it. Berries should be

(continued on page 31)

washed only if needed and patted dry with a paper towel. Strawberries should be hulled. Spread them in a single layer on a tray lined with plastic wrap (to keep them from freezing and sticking to the tray if they are damp). When they are frozen hard (1 to 2 hours), enclose them in heavy plastic bags until you are ready to use them. They will keep for at least 6 months.

about JAM MAKING

If you've never made jam before, don't worry—it is quite easy to do. If the fruit is high in pectin, a natural substance that helps the fruit jell, it can be boiled with a sweetener and a little acid until it reaches a pleasing thickness. If the fruit is low in pectin, powdered or liquid pectin is added to help the jam set. Measure carefully, stir frequently to avoid scorching, and test often to see if the jam has reached the jellying point.

testing for the jellying point is not complicated. Simply place a small spoonful of jam on a cold saucer (I usually put a stack of saucers in the freezer when I begin cooking the jam), and put the saucer in the freezer for about 1 minute. Take it out and draw your finger through the middle of the puddle of jam. If the surface wrinkles and the channel left by your finger stays divided, your jam is ready. If you've already done one test and suspect that your mixture is close to the jellying point, remove it from the heat while you do the test to prevent it from overcooking.

How long it will take to get to the jellying point can vary tremendously from one batch of jam to another. The time is affected by the type of fruit, the variety of fruit, the ripeness of the fruit, even whether the growing season was rainy or not. It will be affected by how well the pot you use conducts heat, what level of heat your stove produces, and whether your pot is low and wide or narrow and high. Because of this variability, I have not given times for cooking the jam until it reaches the jellying point. You will have to be vigilant and start testing once the jam begins to thicken.

Don't forget, you are not making Jell-O. You *should* be able to drizzle homemade jam over a hot biscuit. If the jam is really soupy, put it all back in the pot and cook it a little longer. Conversely, rock-solid jam can be heated with more water to thin it if necessary.

storing JAMS AND MARMALADES

Jam ladled into sterilized jars can be stored in the refrigerator for up to 3 months. **(To sterilize jars, submerge them in boiling water for 10 minutes.)** The boiling water bath method of preserving jam is more practical, however, since the jars will keep at room temperature for up to a year. Neither you nor the recipient of your gift will have to fuss with refrigerator space until the jar is opened. If you are new to jam making, don't be deterred by the number of steps involved in the water bath. The process is relatively short and simple.

presenting JAMS AS GIFTS

When you are formulating a plan for making and wrapping a gift of jam, choosing jars is the first decision you will want to make. Ball jars from your local grocery or hardware store are inexpensive and easy to find. Other fancier jars suitable for canning, like the Weck jars from Germany that are also designed for processing in a boiling water bath, can be found in upscale hardware or housewares stores and in some catalogs. Pretty labels, ribbons, raffia, and whether or not to use paper or fabric covers are among the choices you will make along the way to creating a special gift. See The Art of Giving, page 10, for detailed instructions on making jar covers.

4. When you are ready to fill the jars, drain the hot water from them and fill them to within $1/4$ inch of the top (this is called headspace) with jam, fruit, or pickle. Wipe the top and inside rim of the jar with a clean, damp paper towel before covering the top with the lid. Screw on the bands.

5. With a sturdy pair of tongs, place the jars on a rack or a thick folded dish towel in the pot of boiling water. Process the jars with the water at a gentle boil for the time required in the recipe. If necessary, during processing, add more boiling water to cover the jars by 1 to 2 inches.

6. Remove the jars from the water bath and allow to cool. After 12 hours, check to see that the jars are sealed by pressing on the center of the lid. It should remain concave.

7. Label and date the jars by writing on the lids with a permanent marker.

8. Remove the screw bands to prevent them from rusting on and store the jars for up to 1 year in a cool, dark place. The ideal temperature for storage is 50° to 70°.

blueberry-raspberry JAM

To me, raspberries and blueberries in combination make a more interesting jam than one made with a single type of berry. While I often find that jams made with pectin have a diluted, almost dull flavor and a Jell-O-like texture, this jam is an exception. In fact, it's such a quick, easy recipe with consistently great results that I always recommend it to first-time jam makers. Once you have given away a jar to a friend, however, you may, like me, get frequent requests for more.

4 cups fresh or frozen blueberries (about 2 pints)

4 cups fresh or frozen raspberries (about 2 pints)

5 1/2 cups sugar

2 tablespoons freshly squeezed lemon juice

2 tablespoons water

1 (1.75-ounce) package powdered pectin (Sure-Jell and Certo brands are recommended)

PICK over the berries to remove stems and any soft berries. Measure the sugar and set aside.

COMBINE the berries with the lemon juice, water, and pectin in a 6-quart or larger heavy-bottomed pot. Place over high heat and bring to a hard boil, stirring often. Add the sugar and stir constantly until the mixture returns to a boil. Boil for exactly 1 minute.

LADLE the hot jam into clean, hot jars, leaving a 1/4-inch headspace, seal, and process in a boiling water bath (see page 30) for 10 minutes for long-term storage. Or ladle the jam into sterilized jars, cover, and store in the refrigerator for up to 3 months.

blackberry-peach JAM

▶ MAKES 7 TO 8 HALF-PINT JARS

Here is a combination of fruits that will set your jam apart from anything found on the grocery shelf. Blackberries and peaches are a natural pair: The berries add tartness and a beautiful color to the peaches, and sage leaves lend a certain mysterious quality. Look for slightly underripe blackberries if possible.

4 cups fresh or frozen blackberries (about 2 pints)

Large handful of fresh sage leaves, coarsely chopped

1 cup water

4 pounds perfect peaches

6 cups sugar

PICK over the berries to remove stems and any soft berries. Combine the blackberries, sage leaves, and water in a heavy-bottomed saucepan and bring to a boil. Reduce the heat and simmer until the blackberries are soft and falling apart, about 20 minutes.

SET a fine-mesh strainer over a bowl, and pass the berry mixture through it, pressing to extract as much pulp and juice as possible. Discard the seeds and sage leaves.

BRING a 4-quart or larger pot of water to a boil. Working with 4 or 5 peaches at a time, drop them into the boiling water and blanch for 40 to 50 seconds to loosen the skins. Transfer them with a slotted spoon to a bowl of cold water for another 30 seconds to cool them, and slip off the skins. Slice into eighths, discarding the pits.

PUT the peach slices in a 6-quart or larger heavy-bottomed pot and mash them coarsely with a potato masher. Add the strained blackberry pulp and sugar to the peaches. Gently heat the mixture, stirring occasionally, until the sugar dissolves. Then increase the heat and bring the mixture to a boil. Continue to cook over medium heat, stirring often, until the mixture reaches the jellying point (see page 30; timing will vary).

(continued)

LADLE the hot jam into clean, hot jars, leaving a $1/4$-inch headspace, seal, and process in a boiling water bath (see page 30) for 10 minutes for long-term storage. Or ladle the hot jam into sterilized jars, cover, and store in the refrigerator for up to 3 months.

FREEZING PEACHES

When peaches are available but time to make jam is not, enclose them, whole and unpeeled, in a plastic bag and pop the bag in the freezer. When it comes time to make the jam, remove the peaches from the freezer, spread them on a tray, and leave them to thaw for about 20 minutes. They are easiest to handle when they are partially frozen but not rock solid. Place them in a colander and pour boiling water over them to loosen their skins. Peel, pit, slice, and proceed with recipe.

strawberry **RUBIES**

The French way of making preserves is to preserve spoon-sized fruits whole in a concentrated fruit syrup. In this method, berries are immersed briefly in a boiling sugar syrup. The berries and syrup are then left to cool separately, reunited, and left to stand for a day. The process is repeated three times over a period of 3 days, so that the sugar permeates the berries slowly without mashing the fruit. Finally, the syrup is cooked to the jellying point and the berries are returned to it. Here is a shorter version with similar results—lovely jewels suspended in strawberry syrup. Small, teaspoon-sized berries make the best preserves.

3 pounds fresh strawberries
    (about 2 quarts)

7 cups sugar

Juice of 1 to 2 large lemons
    ($^1/_3$ to $^1/_2$ cup juice)

HULL the strawberries and leave them whole. (Halve or quarter very large berries, if necessary.) Layer the berries in a bowl with half of the sugar and let stand for 2 to 3 hours, until the sugar liquefies and starts to dissolve.

POUR the berries into a colander placed over a 6-quart or larger heavy-bottomed pot, capturing the fruit syrup in the pot. Set the berries aside in the colander over a bowl.

ADD the remaining sugar to the syrup in the pot and bring the mixture to a boil over medium heat, stirring until the sugar dissolves. Add the drained strawberries and any accumulated juices to the pot and return the mixture to a boil. Cook over medium heat for 12 minutes from the time the mixture returns to a boil. Turn off the heat and stir in the lemon juice. Use the larger quantity of juice for very ripe berries.

(continued)

IMMEDIATELY POUR the berry mixture into a large, flat baking dish (a 9 by 13-inch glass baking dish works well). When the berries have cooled, cover with plastic wrap and let stand overnight.

THE NEXT DAY, return the berries and syrup to the same pot, bring to a boil, and cook, stirring often, until the mixture reaches the jellying point (see page 30). This should take from 10 to 15 minutes. Watch carefully and don't over-cook.

LADLE the hot jam into clean, hot jars, leaving a $^1/_4$-inch headspace, seal, and process in a boiling water bath (see page 30) for 10 minutes for long-term storage. Or ladle the hot jam into sterilized jars, cover, and store in the refrigerator for up to 3 months. To keep the strawberries from floating, invert the jars several times while cooling.

plum and lemon JAM

▶ MAKES 8 TO 9 HALF-PINT JARS

The beautiful color of plums combined with the tart and slightly bitter flavor of lemons appeals to jam and marmalade lovers alike. A loaf of simple homemade white bread goes nicely with this gift. Sliced and toasted, it shows off the bright taste and color of the jam. While small red plums or purple Italian prune plums are the easiest to work with, any plum that pleases you will do. If you choose large plums, some pieces may have to be diced.

4 pounds plums

1 cup water

3 small or 2 large lemons

6 cups sugar

COMBINE the plums and water in a heavy-bottomed saucepan and bring to a simmer. Cover partially and simmer over low heat for about 20 minutes, or until tender. Remove from the heat and let stand for several hours (or overnight, if more convenient) until completely cool.

REMOVE the pits from the plums and reserve the plums and their juice. If using large plums, break them up into spoon-sized pieces.

QUARTER THE LEMONS, remove the seeds, and slice the quarters crosswise as thinly as possible. Alternatively, slice the whole lemons in $1/8$-inch-thick rounds, again removing the seeds as you slice. Then chop the slices into small pieces in a food processor with a series of pulses. Take care not to reduce them to a purée.

PLACE the lemon slices or pieces in a saucepan, cover with water, bring to a boil, and simmer, uncovered, for 20 minutes, or until tender. Drain.

COMBINE the plums and their juice, drained lemons, and sugar in a 6-quart or larger heavy-bottomed pot. Gently heat the mixture, stirring occasionally until the sugar dissolves, then increase the heat and bring to a boil. Continue to cook over medium heat, stirring often, until the mixture reaches the jellying point (see page 30; timing will vary).

LADLE the hot jam into clean, hot jars, leaving a $^1/_4$-inch headspace, seal, and process in a boiling water bath (see page 30) for 10 minutes for long-term storage. Or ladle the hot jam into sterilized jars, cover, and store in the refrigerator for up to 3 months.

end-of-summer JAM

▶ MAKES ABOUT 9 HALF-PINT JARS

When September comes and the evening light starts to fade, the impulse to preserve often arises along with thoughts of the winter holidays ahead. What better time to think of putting aside some jars for giving away when the weather is cold? You can't bring back the berry season, but many fruits still await you at the farmers' market, and this jam makes use of them in a lovely combination.

2 pounds peaches

2 pounds pears

2 pounds plums

1 large lemon

$1/2$ cup water

2-inch piece gingerroot

$7 1/2$ cups sugar

BRING a 4-quart or larger pot of water to a boil. Working with 4 or 5 peaches at a time, drop them into the boiling water and blanch for 40 to 50 seconds to loosen the skins. Transfer them with a slotted spoon to a bowl of cold water for another 30 seconds to cool them, and slip off the skins. Slice the peaches, discarding the pits, then cut into $3/4$-inch pieces.

PEEL, core, and dice the pears into similar-sized pieces. Dice the unpeeled plums into the same-sized pieces, discarding the pits.

WITH A ZESTER, remove the zest from the lemon to create thin strips. Halve the lemon and extract the juice, discarding the seeds.

COMBINE the diced fruits, lemon zest, lemon juice, and water in a 6-quart or larger heavy-bottomed pot. Make a few slashes in the gingerroot with a paring knife and add it, in one piece, to the pot. Bring the mixture to a boil and simmer over medium heat for 15 to 20 minutes, until the fruit is tender. Gradually stir in the sugar, 1 cup at a time, and continue to cook over medium heat, stirring often, until the mixture reaches the jellying point (see page 30; timing will vary). Remove and discard the gingerroot.

LADLE the hot jam into clean, hot jars, leaving a $^1/_4$-inch headspace, seal, and process in a boiling water bath (see page 30) for 10 minutes for long-term storage. Or ladle into sterilized jars, cover, and store in the refrigerator for up to 3 months.

blood orange MARMALADE

▶ MAKES ABOUT 10 HALF-PINT JARS

Blood oranges are delightfully dramatic and, fortunately, much easier to find now than in the past, although the season remains limited to a few short weeks in late winter. They cry out to be used, even preserved. Here is a deep amber marmalade, perfect for Valentine's Day. If blood oranges are not in the market, substitute navel or Valencia oranges.

Total of 4 pounds of fruit consisting of 8 to 9 blood oranges and 2 to 3 lemons

12 cups water

8 cups sugar

PLACE the fruit in a 6-quart or larger heavy-bottomed pot and cover with the water. Cover the pot, bring to a boil, decrease the heat to low, and simmer for 25 to 35 minutes, until the fruit is tender when pierced with a fork. Remove the pot from the heat and let stand for several hours (or overnight if more convenient) until completely cool.

WITH A SLOTTED SPOON, remove the fruit from the cooking liquid. Reserve $3^1/_2$ cups of the liquid in the pot, discarding the remainder.

QUARTER the fruits through the stem ends and cut crosswise into very thin slices, discarding the seeds.

RETURN the sliced fruits to the pot with the reserved cooking liquid and the sugar. Gently heat the mixture, stirring occasionally until the sugar dissolves, then increase the heat and bring to a boil. Continue to cook over medium heat, stirring often, until the mixture reaches the jellying point (see page 30; timing will vary).

LADLE the hot marmalade into clean, hot jars, leaving a $^1/_4$-inch headspace, seal, and process in a boiling water bath (page 30) for 10 minutes for long-term storage. Or ladle the hot jam into sterilized jars, cover, and store in the refrigerator for up to 3 months.

Irish Whiskey Marmalade
In this version, the alcohol taste evaporates, leaving behind the rich depth of the whiskey flavor. Follow the above recipe, using blood, navel, or Valencia oranges, or bitter Seville oranges if you can find them. Put 1 to 2 tablespoons of whiskey in the bottom of each jar and fill with marmalade as directed.

clementine-cranberry MARMALADE

▶ MAKES 8 TO 9 HALF-PINT JARS

Just when you think it's too late to make jam, clementines and cranberries show up in the market, presenting you with another opportunity to create a special Christmas gift. If you've already gone the fruitcake or Christmas cookie route, you'll want to try this recipe. Pack a jar of the marmalade together with a tin of a tea from Great Britain and some homemade scones.

3 pounds clementines (14 to 16)

2 lemons

2 1/2 cups water

3 whole cloves

2-inch-long cinnamon stick

4 whole allspice berries

2 thin slices gingerroot

3 1/2 cups sugar

1/2 cup dried currants

2 cups fresh cranberries, picked over

SCRUB the clementines and lemons. If they are not organic, immerse them in boiling water for 30 seconds to remove any pesticides and wax. Cool in a bowl of ice water.

HALVE the clementines and lemons through the stem ends. Place the halves flat side down on a cutting board, and slice them as thinly as possible, discarding the seeds.

IN A 6-QUART or larger heavy-bottomed pot, combine the clementines, lemons, and water. Bring to a boil and cook, uncovered, over medium heat for about 15 minutes, or until fruit is tender.

TIE the cloves, cinnamon stick, allspice berries, and gingerroot in a cheesecloth bag and add it to the pot along with the sugar. Slowly return the mixture to a boil. Continue to cook over medium heat, stirring often, until the mixture reaches the jellying point (see page 30; timing will vary).

REMOVE the spice bag and stir in the currants and cranberries. Return the mixture to a boil and boil for 1 minute.

LADLE the hot marmalade into clean, hot jars, leaving a 1/4-inch headspace, seal, and process in a boiling water bath (see page 30) for 10 minutes for long-term storage. Or ladle the hot jam into sterilized jars, cover, and store in the refrigerator for up to 3 months.

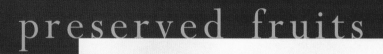
preserved fruits

chapter four

Classic Gifts

ike jams, preserved fruits are wonderful plan-ahead gifts to make. When the holiday crush begins, the cook who has some special jars of preserved fruit on the shelf can be at home relaxing or writing a few cards while everyone else is out shopping. And no store or catalog can supply you with such lovely, unique gifts. The sheer pleasure of home-canned peaches had escaped me until a friend gave me a jar as a gift. Now I don't let peach season go by without putting up some jars for myself and my friends. What better way to welcome a new family to your neighborhood than with a basket of breakfast foods that includes Blueberry-Lemon Sauce or home-canned peaches. They can put these treats aside until they have settled in and are ready for their first Sunday morning feast in their new home. The other fruits in this chapter, like Pears in Red Wine and Plums in Plum Liqueur, are elegant enough to take to a dinner party, to be consumed that evening or to be put away for a future meal.

Because these fruits look so beautiful in their jars, they should have minimal wrapping. A pretty label, a wide satin ribbon tied around the neck, or a simple jar cover with a label and serving suggestions attached is all that is needed for embellishment. See The Art of Giving, page 10, for step-by-step instructions on making jar covers.

blueberry-lemon SAUCE

▶ MAKES 3 PINT JARS

This sauce makes a nice gift in a bountiful breakfast basket or simply paired with a package of pancake mix. You could suggest serving it over ice cream or on cheesecake, too. Dainty, delicious Maine blueberries are especially nice to use here. If you have missed blueberry season, try making it with frozen berries. The recipe can be doubled or halved with good results.

8 cups fresh or frozen blueberries (about 4 pints)

1 lemon

1 to 1 1/4 cups sugar

1/2 cup orange juice

PICK over the blueberries to remove stems and any soft berries.

WITH A HANDHELD GRATER, finely grate the zest from the lemon. Halve the lemon and extract the juice, discarding the seeds.

COMBINE the lemon zest, lemon juice, 1 cup sugar, orange juice, and blueberries in a 4-quart or larger heavy-bottomed pot. Bring the mixture to a boil, stirring occasionally to dissolve the sugar. Decrease the heat and simmer for 1 or 2 minutes to dissolve the sugar thoroughly. Taste and add up to 1/4 cup more sugar if the berries are very tart.

LADLE the hot sauce into clean, hot jars, leaving a 1/4-inch headspace, seal, and process in a boiling water bath (see page 30) for 10 minutes for long-term storage. Or ladle the sauce into sterilized jars, cover, and refrigerate for up to 3 months.

home-canned PEACHES
in a LIGHT LEMON SYRUP

▶ MAKES 6 QUART JARS

Home-canned peaches are a revelation: light and tart and juicy. Until I tasted some that a friend brought along for breakfast, I confess that I never was inspired to try any sort of canning. Now, thanks to these wondrous peaches, I've got the canning bug. A jar of these golden peaches makes a fine gift alone, but you could pair it with a bag of granola or muffin mix, too. This is one gift I practically have to sneak out of the house, or suffer a jealous outcry from my family.

For variety, add some almond extract—and almond liqueur, if you like—or a few slices of fresh ginger to the sugar syrup. February mornings are a lot less dreary with a jar of home-canned peaches on the table.

1 lemon

3 cups sugar

6 cups water

10 to 12 pounds perfect peaches

Fruit protector powder, or juice of
   1 lemon

USING A VEGETABLE PEELER, remove the zest in $1/2$-inch strips, being careful to leave behind the bitter white pith. Cut the lemon in half, extract the juice, then strain the juice, discarding the seeds and pulp.

COMBINE the lemon zest, lemon juice, sugar, and water in a large saucepan and bring to a boil, stirring until the sugar is completely dissolved. Lift out the lemon zest with a slotted spoon and set aside. Leave the sugar syrup in the pan.

BRING a 4-quart or larger pot of water to a boil. Halve each peach by cutting along the "crease" through to the pit. Twist the halves gently in opposite directions to release them from the pit, then remove the pit with a teaspoon. Working with 4 or 5 peaches at a time, drop the halves into the boiling water and blanch for 40 to 50 seconds to loosen the skins. Transfer them with a slotted spoon to a bowl of cold water for another 30 seconds to cool, and slip off

(continued)

the skins. Finally, drop them into a large bowl of cold water treated with fruit protector powder or acidulated with the lemon juice.

WHEN all of the peaches are peeled, pack the halves into clean, hot quart jars with the flat sides down, overlapping them in layers and alternating with a few pieces of reserved lemon zest in each jar.

BRING the syrup back to a boil and pour it over the peaches, leaving a $^1/_2$-inch headspace. Gently slip a wooden skewer or chopstick between the fruit and the side of each jar to release air bubbles. Seal and process in a boiling water bath (see page 30) for 25 minutes for long-term storage. Store the peaches away from light in a cool place for up to 1 year.

FRUIT PROTECTOR POWDER

Fruit protector powder is a commercial product made of citric and ascorbic acids and is available in the canning section of most supermarkets. It is used to prevent home-canned fruit from darkening in the jar over time. Directions for its use are provided by the manufacturer.

peaches in **RASPBERRY CHAMPAGNE**

▶ MAKES 3 QUART JARS

This is a classic, classy combination for a dessert in a jar. Your friend who entertains often will love to receive these peaches, alone or paired with a package of small, crisp cookies. Suggest serving them chilled in shallow dessert bowls, surrounded by the sauce and topped with a dollop of crème fraîche and a smattering of toasted sliced almonds. Use an inexpensive but drinkable, dry champagne-style (sparkling) wine, or substitute a Sauvignon Blanc. The recipe can be doubled to make 6 quarts.

3 cups fresh raspberries
(about 1^1/$_2$ pints)

1^1/$_2$ cups sugar

3 or 4 sprigs tarragon

1 (750-ml) bottle dry champagne

5 to 6 pounds perfect peaches

Fruit protector powder, or juice of
1 lemon

6 tablespoons framboise or other
fruit liqueur (optional)

PICK over the raspberries and discard any soft ones. Combine the raspberries, sugar, and tarragon in a 4-quart or larger heavy-bottomed pot and heat until the sugar and berries liquefy, mashing the berries against the side of the pot with a wooden spoon.

ADD the champagne and bring to a boil, stirring vigilantly to prevent the mixture from boiling over, as it will explode in bubbles when it heats up. Simmer for a minute or two, until the major bubble explosion subsides. Turn off the heat and let the mixture steep while you prepare the peaches.

BRING a 4-quart or larger pot of water to a boil. Halve each peach by cutting along the "crease" through to the pit. Twist the halves gently in opposite directions to release them from the pit, then remove the pit with a teaspoon. Working with 4 to 5 peaches at a time, drop the halves into the boiling water and blanch for 40 to 50 seconds to loosen the skins. Transfer them with a slotted spoon to a bowl of cold water for another 30 seconds to cool, and slip off the skins. Finally, drop them into a large bowl of cold water treated with fruit protector powder or acidulated with the lemon juice.

(continued)

LINE a strainer with a double layer of dampened cheesecloth and set it over a bowl. Pour the raspberry liquid through it, pressing to extract as much juice as possible. Discard the pulp, tarragon, and seeds. Return the syrup to the pan.

PACK the peach halves into clean, hot quart jars with the flat sides down, over-lapping them in layers to fill the jars a little more than three-quarters full. Add 2 tablespoons fruit liqueur to each jar.

BRING the raspberry syrup back to a boil and pour it over the peaches, leaving a $^1/_2$-inch headspace. Gently slip a wooden skewer or chopstick between the fruit and the side of each jar to release air bubbles. Seal and process in a boiling water bath for 25 minutes (see page 30) for long-term storage. Store the peaches away from light in a cool place for up to 1 year, although the beautiful raspberry color may begin to fade after about 6 months.

pears in **RED WINE**

No ordinary gift, these pears have an earthy elegance imparted by the smoky caramel in their deep-red wine sauce. Your weekend host or hostess will appreciate having a jar on hand to augment one of the many meals that will be served. A tag on the jar could suggest serving the pears warm with honey ice cream or unsweetened whipped cream. Or you could bring along a bag of your favorite chocolate cookies from the bakery.

Bartlett pears of uniform size are ideal, but you could use Bosc, Comice, or even whole Seckel pears. They should be unblemished and firm. Slightly underripe pears are best. Choose a simple Côtes de Rhône or any dry, fruity wine for the poaching liquid. The recipe can be doubled.

2 cups sugar

Juice of $1/2$ lemon

2 (750-ml) bottles red wine

6 pounds Bartlett or other firm pears

2 vanilla beans

$1/2$ teaspoon black peppercorns

8 bay leaves

TO MAKE THE CARAMEL, combine the sugar and lemon juice in a heavy-bottomed saucepan. Mix with your fingers until the sugar is completely saturated with the lemon. (The acid in the lemon keeps the caramel from crystallizing.) Stir with a wooden spoon over medium heat until the mixture liquefies and turns a deep amber. Turn off the heat and stir the caramel briefly to cool it slightly. It should remain liquid.

VERY CAREFULLY POUR about 2 cups of the wine, a little at a time, into the hot caramel. The mixture may splatter and bubble, so stand back and use caution. If bits of caramel harden, simply return the mixture to the heat and stir until they dissolve. Transfer the wine syrup to a 6-quart or larger pot (large enough to accommodate the pears) and add the remaining wine.

(continued)

CARAMEL CAUTION

Use a long-handled wooden spoon and an oven mitt for stirring the caramel. The sugar gets very, very hot and can give you a nasty burn if you are not careful.

PEEL and halve the pears through the stem ends, leaving the stems intact if you like. Remove the cores and blossom ends with a melon baller. Drop the pears into the wine syrup as you work.

RETURN the syrup to a boil, reduce the heat, and simmer the pears for about 10 minutes, or until they feel tender when pierced with the point of a knife. With a wooden spoon, gently transfer the pears to a colander set over a bowl. Let cool for a few minutes while you reduce the wine.

SPLIT the vanilla beans in half lengthwise and, using the tip of a knife, scrape the seeds into the wine mixture. Add the vanilla pods, peppercorns, and bay leaves and any accumulated liquid from the draining pears. Bring the mixture to a vigorous boil and boil briskly for 15 to 20 minutes, until it looks syrupy and has reduced to about $4^1/_2$ cups. Pour the syrup through a fine-mesh strainer lined with cheesecloth or a paper towel placed over a saucepan. Keep hot.

WHEN the pear halves are cool enough to handle, pack them into clean, hot quart jars with the flat sides down, overlapping them in layers to fill the jars about three-quarters full. Reheat the syrup, if necessary, then pour the hot syrup over the pears, leaving a $^1/_2$-inch headspace. Slip a wooden skewer or chopstick gently between the fruit and the side of each jar to release air bubbles. Seal and process in a boiling water bath (see page 30) for 25 minutes for long-term storage. Store the pears away from light in a cool place for up to 1 year.

cherry and apricot **COMPOTE**

Luscious cherries and apricots come our way for such a short season that it seems criminal not to do something to preserve them. And that is just what makes this compote a gift to be treasured. Suggest serving it chilled with whipped cream or over a dish of vanilla ice cream. Be sure to use perfectly ripe, unblemished fruit, but err on the side of slightly underripe if necessary.

$^1/_2$ **pound dried apricots**

4 cups water

2 pounds fresh apricots

2 pounds dark, sweet cherries

2 large lemons

1 cup sugar

6 tablespoons amaretto (almond liqueur)

1 teaspoon pure almond extract

CUT the dried apricots into $^1/_4$-inch-thick matchsticks. You should have about $1^1/_2$ cups. Combine them in a saucepan with the water and bring to a boil. Turn off the heat and let the apricots stand in the water while you prepare the rest of the fruit.

QUARTER the fresh apricots through the stem ends (or cut into sixths if the apricots are large), discarding the pits. You do not need to peel them.

REMOVE the stems and pits from the cherries. You can leave the cherries whole by using a cherry pitter or you can halve them with a knife to remove the pits.

USING A HANDHELD GRATER, finely grate the zest from the lemons. Halve the lemons and extract the juice, discarding the seeds.

DRAIN the soaked apricots, reserving 2 cups of the soaking liquid. Combine the reserved liquid with the lemon zest, lemon juice, and sugar in a large, heavy-bottomed pot. Stir over medium heat until the sugar dissolves and the syrup comes to a boil.

ADD the drained apricot pieces, the fresh apricot pieces, and the cherries to the syrup. Return the mixture to a full boil, and boil gently for 2 to 3 minutes,

(continued)

until fruit is hot all the way through. Turn off the heat and stir in the amaretto and the almond extract.

USING a slotted spoon, transfer the hot fruits to clean, hot jars, filling them to within $1/2$ inch of the top. Pour in the hot syrup to cover, leaving a $1/4$-inch headspace. Seal and process in a boiling water bath for 10 minutes (see page 30) for long-term storage. Or spoon the fruit into sterilized jars, add the hot syrup, cover, and store in the refrigerator for up to 3 weeks.

CANNING JARS

When using pint canning jars, note that wide-mouthed Ball jars and "regular" (smaller-mouthed) jars hold exactly the same amount, but the wide-mouthed jars look much bigger and are easier to fill.

<h1>plums in PLUM LIQUEUR</h1>

▶ MAKES ABOUT 3 PINT OR HALF-LITER JARS

These plums come from a long tradition of preserving fruits in brandy or other spirits. Country housewives in France have been making them for at least a century, for their own households or to give as gifts.

French or Italian preserving jars with metal clamps and rubber rims make the prettiest containers for these plums. Tie a ribbon or piece of raffia around the jar and attach a hand-written label on a piece of nice paper to suggest serving them individually in small wine-glasses surrounded by the liqueur or over ice cream. A jar makes a wonderful gift by itself or paired with a package of biscotti or other small cookies.

Small plums—just slightly larger than walnuts—are essential to a pretty result. Italian prune plums are the easiest to find, but once I came across a display of "French" prune plums at a farm stand. They were a dusky rose and shaped like small figs. In this recipe, the trick is to boil the plums without tearing the skins too much and turning the whole thing into a mush. Cooking the plums in one layer and using a wooden spoon to push them around in the syrup minimize breakage.

The recipe doubles or triples nicely. Just cook and "rest" the plums in one layer as directed for the smaller quantity.

2 1/2 pounds small Italian prune plums

2 cups sugar

1 cup water

2-inch-long cinnamon stick

5 whole cloves

About 1 1/2 cups good-quality vodka

PRICK each plum 2 or 3 times with a darning needle.

COMBINE the sugar and water in a high-sided 10-inch skillet and bring to a boil, stirring until the sugar dissolves. Add half of the plums to the syrup; they should fit comfortably in the pan in one layer. Return the syrup to a boil and cook, pushing the plums around in the syrup with a wooden spoon, for 2 to 3 minutes. With a slotted spoon, gently transfer the plums to a 9 by 13-inch glass baking dish. Repeat with the remaining plums.

(continued)

POUR the hot syrup over the plums, now in a single layer in the baking dish, and cover immediately with a sheet of plastic wrap. Leave the plums overnight in the syrup, turning them once or twice.

WITH THE SLOTTED SPOON, transfer the plums to sterilized jars, filling the jars about three-quarters full. Transfer the syrup to a saucepan, add the cinnamon stick and cloves, and bring to a boil. Continue to boil until slightly thickened. You should have about $1^1/_2$ cups.

STRAIN the hot syrup through a fine-mesh strainer, and then pour it over the plums, filling each jar about one-half full. Let cool and pour in the vodka. The liquid should cover the plums completely. Seal the jars, label, and store in a cool, dark place. Leave to rest for at least 2 months before opening or giving away. Gently tilt the jars every so often to mix the syrup and the vodka. The plums will keep almost indefinitely.

MATCHES MADE IN HEAVEN (AND IN YOUR KITCHEN)

Blueberry-Lemon Sauce (page 48) and pancake mix (pages 20 to 22)

Home-Canned Peaches in Light Lemon Syrup (page 49) and Maple-Cranberry Granola (page 24)

Cherry and Apricot Compote (page 57) and Hazelnut Shortbread (page 113)

Peaches in Raspberry Champagne (page 51) and Palets de Dames (page 112)

Pears in Red Wine (page 54) and Triple-Chocolate Walnut Cookies (page 124)

Plums in Plum Liqueur (page 59) and Ginger Pennies (page 118)

homemade liqueurs

chapter five

Bottled Luxury

My love affair with liqueurs started with a gift of framboise from a French neighbor. One sip of this intense berry elixir gave me a glimpse of something new. Suddenly I understood a different way of life, a life where people sit at tables under shade trees and enjoy glasses of grandmother's cordial and one another's company. Well, we can't all live in the south of France, but we can make special liqueurs to give to our friends and look forward to sharing some convivial moments with them.

Recipes for fruit liqueurs are stunningly simple. Add liquor and sugar to fruit, wait a month or two, strain, and bottle. You could make a family outing of picking berries or buy them at a farm stand or urban greenmarket. Once you add the prescribed alcohol, you can pretty much forget about them until you're ready to bottle.

The recipes that follow are designed to go into recycled wine bottles that hold 750 milliliters, or about 3 cups. Clear bottles that usually hold rosé wines are the best. I've been known to buy a wine just for the pretty bottle. Soak off the label and scrape away any stubborn bits of paper with a knife. Wash well and drain thoroughly. If you see special bottles in a catalog or a gift shop, by all means plan to use them. Do not worry if their capacity does not conform exactly to the recipe. Your gift can be any size you choose. If there's a bit left over for you, the cook, to keep in your cupboard, all the better.

You'll find plain new corks in hardware stores, but you may find unusual decorative corks in gift catalogs or fancy kitchen supply stores.

Like preserved fruits, bottles of these liqueurs are beautiful enough to require only pretty labels and perhaps ribbon or raffia wrapped around the neck. For step-by-step instructions on sealing and dipping the cork in colored wax, refer to The Art of Giving, page 14.

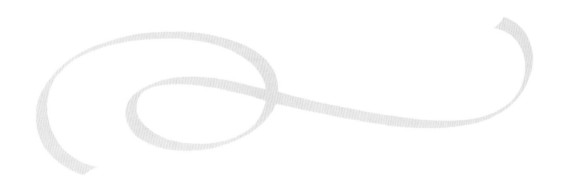

FRAMBOISE

*This exquisite liqueur has become the cornerstone of my own holiday gift-giving reper-
toire. I usually make a lot of it, enough for three wine bottles and a little for myself.
The recipe can be halved if you want to make less. The vodka you use should be of
decent, drinkable quality.*

(pictured, page 66, right)

**6 cups fresh raspberries
(about 3 pints)**

12 cups good-quality vodka

3 cups sugar

1 1/2 cups water

PICK over the raspberries and discard any soft ones. Place the raspberries in a
clean 4-quart glass jar. Add the vodka, cover with a lid, and let steep for about
2 months in a cool, dark place. Stir every few weeks.

LINE a large strainer with a triple layer of dampened cheesecloth and set it over
a bowl. Strain the mixture through it. Bring the corners of the cheesecloth
together to make a bag. Twist the ends and squeeze to extract as much liquid
as possible. Discard the pulp.

WASH the jar and return the liquid to it. Let stand for about 2 hours. If there
is sediment at the bottom of the jar, pour off all the clear liquid into a clean
container and filter the remaining cloudy liquid through a coffee filter, changing the filter occasionally to speed up the straining process.

COMBINE the sugar and water in a saucepan and bring to a boil over medium
heat. Boil, stirring, for 1 to 2 minutes, until the sugar is dissolved. Allow to
cool to room temperature.

ADD about 1 3/4 cups of the sugar syrup to the liqueur and taste. If necessary,
add more, about 1/4 cup at a time, until you arrive at a satisfactory sweetness.
The amount of sugar syrup will depend on your taste buds and the sweetness
of the raspberries.

POUR the liqueur into clean, dry bottles and cork them. Drink within a year,
before the color and flavor fade.

orange RATAFIA

▶ MAKES ENOUGH TO FILL 2 WINE BOTTLES, OR ABOUT 6 CUPS

The intense orange and herbal notes of this sweet flavored brandy are meant to be enjoyed as a bracing aperitif over ice, or as a pleasant after-dinner digestif *served at room temperature in small cordial glasses. Use a moderately priced domestic brandy with a smooth finish.*

(pictured, page 66, left)

6 oranges

1¹/₂ cups sugar

1 cup (about 4 ounces) coriander
    seeds

4 cups brandy

USING A VEGETABLE PEELER, remove the zest from the oranges, being careful to leave behind the bitter white pith. Cut the oranges in half and extract the juice, discarding the seeds.

COMBINE the orange zest, orange juice, sugar, coriander, and brandy in a large glass jar. Cover the jar with a lid and let steep for 2 months in a cool, dark place. Stir every few weeks.

LINE a large strainer with a double layer of dampened cheesecloth and set it over a bowl. Strain the mixture through it and press to extract as much liquid as possible. Discard the orange zest and seeds.

WASH the jar and return the liquid to it. Allow the ratafia to stand undisturbed for several hours or overnight. If there is sediment at the bottom of the jar, pour off all the clear liquid into a clean container and filter the remaining cloudy liquid through a coffee filter, changing the filter occasionally to speed up the straining process.

POUR the ratafia into clean, dry bottles and cork them. Drink within a year, before the flavor fades.

sweet blackberry WINE

► MAKES ENOUGH TO FILL 2 WINE BOTTLES, OR 6 TO 7 CUPS

(pictured, page 69, right)

Good medicine to drive away the early dark on a brisk autumn afternoon, this sweet wine is a cross between a wine and a liqueur. Suggest serving it after dinner with a fruit dessert or a few cookies, or sipping it by the fire to remember summer.

Use a dry, fruity red wine. A soft Merlot makes a fine choice. You may need to adjust the quantity of sugar according to taste if the berries are very tart.

4 cups fresh blackberries
(about 2 pints)

³/₄ cup granulated sugar

¹/₄ cup water

1 vanilla bean, cut crosswise into
3 pieces

1 cup good-quality vodka

5 cups red wine (about 1¹/₂ bottles)

Superfine sugar (optional)

PICK over the blackberries to remove any stems and soft berries. Combine the blackberries, granulated sugar, water, and vanilla bean in a saucepan. Bring slowly to a simmer, stirring until the sugar is dissolved. Simmer, stirring occasionally, for 10 to 15 minutes, until the berries are soft and falling apart. Remove from the heat and let cool.

STIR in the vodka and red wine. Pour into a clean 4-quart glass jar. Cover the jar with a lid and let steep for 6 to 8 weeks in a cool, dark place. Stir every few weeks.

LINE a large strainer with a triple layer of dampened cheesecloth and set it over a bowl. Strain the mixture through it. Bring the corners of the cheesecloth together to make a bag. Twist the ends and squeeze to extract as much juice as possible. Discard the blackberry pulp, seeds, and vanilla bean. Taste for sweetness and add a few tablespoons of superfine sugar, if you like, stirring to dissolve.

POUR the wine into clean, dry bottles and cork them. Drink within a year, before the flavor fades.

strawberry CORDIAL

▶ MAKES ENOUGH TO FILL 2 WINE BOTTLES, OR ABOUT 6 CUPS

(pictured, page 69, left)

Although this cordial is quite sweet, it is not cloyingly so. The hint of basil adds a distinctive twist. If you have picked your own strawberries and made this in June, it will be ready to give away just when there's a nip in the air—a lovely gift to enjoy while reflecting on the passing season.

Look for ripe, bruise-free strawberries. Since the berries float, you must weight them down until they are saturated with the sugar. The container you choose must be wide enough to accommodate a weight to submerge the berries. I like to use a wide-mouthed glass flour canister with a small saucer to macerate the berries. A pickling crock could also be used.

8 cups fresh strawberries
(about 2 quarts)

Leaves from 2 large sprigs basil

1¹/₂ cups granulated sugar

3³/₄ cups good-quality vodka

Superfine sugar (optional)

HULL the strawberries and discard any soft ones.

PLACE the basil leaves in the bottom of a clean, glass or ceramic, wide-mouthed jar or canister. Add the berries and the granulated sugar in layers. Pour in the vodka to cover by about 1 inch. Weight the berries down and seal the jar with a layer of plastic wrap and the lid. Let steep for about 2 months, tilting the jar every week or so to distribute the sugar (it will melt eventually).

LINE a large strainer with a triple layer of dampened cheesecloth and set it over a bowl. Strain the mixture through it. Bring the corners of the cheesecloth together to make a bag. Twist the ends and squeeze to extract as much liquid as possible. Discard the pulp.

WASH the jar and return the liquid to it. Let stand for about 2 hours. If there is sediment at the bottom of the jar, pour off all the clear liquid into a clean container and filter the remaining cloudy liquid through a coffee filter, changing filters occasionally to speed up the straining process. Taste for sweetness and add a few spoonfuls of superfine sugar, if you like, stirring to dissolve.

POUR the cordial into clean, dry bottles and cork them. Drink within a year, before the color and flavor fade.

FOR THE BRIDE AND GROOM

Two antique cordial glasses and a bottle of your own fruit liqueur make a special gift for a couple's wedding anniversary or for a pair of newlyweds.

condiments

chapter six

*A Savory Jar for
Every Occasion*

*L*et's face it. From time to time we all get weary of our own cooking. That's just why a friend would welcome a little jar of
home-dried tomatoes or preserved lemons for inspiration. With a
gift of perky pickles or homemade chutney to put on the plate, leftovers are
not so dull. Like jams and fruit preserves, condiments you make yourself are
unique. You've chosen the perfect, organic ingredients at the peak of perfection to create a preservative-free product not available in any gourmet-food
catalog. Lucky indeed are the recipients of such gifts.

When wrapping the jars and bottles in this chapter, think in terms of garden colors: a fiery red jar cover for a spicy sauce, a muted sage green for
pickles, a pretty peach or cranberry for chutney. Whether you're using tissue
or covering the jar tops in paper or cloth, consider making a special tag in the
shape of the vegetable or fruit contained in the jar. A pepper cutout for hot
sauces, or a yellow lemon-shaped tag for preserved lemons, adds a little snap
to an already spicy gift. If uses for the gift or serving suggestions are not
immediately evident, be sure to include them on the tag.

basic HERBAL VINEGAR

WHETHER you grow herbs in your garden, or just hate to say good-bye to summer, making flavored vinegar answers the call to preserve without the need for
intensive labor. The herbs look pretty in the bottle, and you don't have to
break a sweat to produce a gift that will please you and the recipient. Kitchen
and hardware stores often have a supply of relatively inexpensive, attractive
bottles and corks. You need only to add a pretty label, a tag suggesting your
favorite uses, and perhaps a bottle of good olive oil. For a finishing touch, read
about dipping the tops of the bottles in colored wax in The Art of Giving,
page 14.

When infusing vinegar with herbs, it is important to have enough herbs to
impart sufficient flavor. Plan on $^1/_2$ cup fresh herb leaves for every 2 cups
vinegar. Steep the leaves in the vinegar for 2 weeks at room temperature,
taste, and strain if it is to your liking, or leave to steep a little longer for a
stronger flavor. When the vinegar has achieved the flavor you want, strain it
through a double layer of cheesecloth into a clean bottle, discard the leaves,
insert 1 to 2 new herb sprigs, and cork.

The best herbs for vinegar are those with sturdy leaves like thyme, rosemary, oregano, or tarragon. Softer-leaved herbs like basil, parsley, and chervil
do not hold up well when left in the bottle. If you wish to use them, simply
discard them after infusing the vinegar, strain the vinegar well, and don't add
fresh herbs to the bottle. Herbs can be used singly or in combination. Peppercorns of various colors, peeled garlic cloves, or a strip or two of lemon or
orange zest can be added for additional interest.

My favorite approach to making herbal vinegar is to shop for a simple
clear glass bottle, fill it neatly with as many branches of the sturdy-leaved herbs
of my choice as will fit, and add white wine vinegar. In 2 weeks it's ready to
go. Although white wine vinegar shows off your herb sprigs best, you can use
red wine vinegar, too.

chile de árbol **SALSA**

► MAKES ABOUT 4 HALF-PINT JARS

Some like it hot, and this sauce is for them. It is meant to be served over broiled meat, in tacos, or with eggs and tortillas for breakfast. A little bit goes a long way. This is a great gift for the barbecue aficionado on your list.

For a slightly different flavor, use 8 to 12 chipotle chiles (smoke-dried jalapeños) in place of the small and fiery chiles de árbol.

2 pounds tomatillos, preferably large ones, husked and well rinsed

18 to 20 dried chiles de árbol

Boiling water to cover

8 cloves garlic, unpeeled

1 teaspoon salt

About 1 cup cold water

8 tablespoons bottled lemon juice

PREHEAT the broiler.

SPREAD the tomatillos on a broiling pan lined with aluminum foil. Slip them under the broiler and broil, turning once, for about 10 minutes, or until they are soft and slightly blackened on both sides. Remove from the broiler and let the tomatillos cool on the pan.

SET an ungreased cast-iron skillet over medium-high heat. When hot, toast the chiles in the pan, turning them, for 1 to 3 minutes, until they are fragrant and make a little crackling sound. Remove from the heat and, when cool enough to handle, discard the stems and seeds.

CRUMBLE the chiles into a small bowl and cover them with boiling water. Let stand for about 20 minutes, or until soft.

MEANWHILE, toast the unpeeled garlic as you did the chiles, in a cast-iron skillet over medium-high heat, turning occasionally, for about 5 minutes, or until soft. Black spots are okay. Remove from the pan and, when cool enough to handle, peel off the skins.

(continued)

DRAIN the chiles, discarding the soaking liquid. Working in batches, combine the chiles, garlic, tomatillos and any accumulated juices from the pan, and the salt in a blender. Purée to a relatively smooth consistency and thin with the cold water to a good consistency. Taste and add more salt if needed. There will be small pieces of chile and seeds from the tomatillo, so the salsa will not look absolutely smooth.

TRANSFER the salsa to a nonreactive saucepan and bring to a boil. Assemble clean, hot jars and add 2 tablespoons of the lemon juice to each one. Ladle the hot salsa into the jars, leaving a $1/4$-inch headspace, seal, and process in a boiling water bath (see page 30) for 20 minutes for long-term storage. Or combine the lemon juice and hot salsa in sterilized jars, cover, and store in the refrigerator for up to 2 weeks.

cascabel CHILE SALSA

▶ MAKES 5 OR 6 HALF-PINT JARS

This barbecue lover's favorite is not quite as hot as the Chile de Árbol Salsa (page 75), but you can get tripped up by a batch of extra-hot chiles every once in awhile. Cascabels look like very large, fat, brown cherries. The sauce is a natural to serve over grilled meats or in tacos, but you could also suggest serving it simply as a dip for tortilla chips. Toasting chiles fills your house with a wonderful aroma, but it can make your eyes burn like crazy. Be sure to open all the windows!

14 dried cascabel chiles

3 pounds ripe tomatoes

3 cloves garlic, thinly sliced

1 teaspoon salt

10 or 12 tablespoons bottled lemon juice

PREHEAT the broiler.

SEPARATE the seeds from the chiles, reserving the seeds. Discard the stems and ribs.

SET an ungreased cast-iron skillet over medium-high heat. When hot, toast the chile seeds for 1 to 2 minutes, or until they are golden brown and start to pop. Pour the seeds into a bowl and set aside.

IN THE SAME SKILLET, toast the chiles, turning them once or twice, for 1 to 3 minutes, until they are fragrant and brown. Remove from the heat and, when cool enough to handle, crumble into a small bowl. Cover them with boiling water and let stand for about 20 minutes, or until soft.

MEANWHILE, core the tomatoes and spread them on a broiler pan lined with aluminum foil. Slip them under the broiler and broil, turning as necessary, until the skins are slightly charred and the tomatoes are soft. Remove from the broiler and let the tomatoes cool on the pan.

DRAIN the chiles and discard the soaking liquid. Working in batches, combine the chiles, chile seeds, tomatoes and any accumulated pan juices, garlic, and salt in a blender. Pulse to chop all the ingredients, but do not purée too smoothly. The texture should be rough. Taste and adjust the amount of salt.

TRANSFER the salsa to a nonreactive saucepan and bring to a boil. Assemble clean, hot jars and add 2 tablespoons of the lemon juice to each one. Ladle the hot salsa into the jars, leaving a $1/4$-inch headspace, seal, and process in a boiling water bath (see page 30) for 20 minutes for long-term storage. Or combine the lemon juice and hot salsa in sterilized jars, cover, and store in the refrigerator for up to 2 weeks.

TOASTING CHILES

The technique of cooking garlic, tomatoes, peppers, and chiles on a hot griddle or over a grill is a signature of Mexican cuisine. It serves to concentrate the flavors of the vegetables and adds a hint of smoke, too. Toasting dried chiles before using intensifies their flavor and prepares them for soaking. Heat an ungreased griddle or cast-iron skillet over medium-high heat. Break the stems off the chiles, lay the chiles in the hot pan, and press them flat with a metal spatula. After a minute or so they will start to crackle. Continue toasting, turning often, for 1 to 3 minutes, until they give off a pleasant smoky fragrance. Remove them from the heat. When cool enough to handle, discard the seeds, if desired, and crumble.

FEARLESS FIRE EATERS

For the fearless fire eaters on your list, pack together a jar of your homemade Pickled Jalapeños (page 82), Chile de Árbol Salsa (page 75), some tortilla chips, and a six-pack of Dos Equis to wash it all down.

green cherry TOMATO PICKLES

▶ MAKES 4 PINT JARS

If you've never made pickles, you will be surprised to discover how easy this recipe is. Gardeners always have abundant supplies of green tomatoes. Ask a friend for some if you don't have a garden of your own, and return the favor with a jar of your pickles and a nice wedge of Cheddar to go with them. For a homey look, make a jar cover with a square of brown paper and tie it up with straw-colored raffia or string.

2 pounds green cherry tomatoes (about 7 cups)

2 small shallots

4 cloves garlic

2 bay leaves, torn into small pieces

1½ teaspoons coriander seeds

1½ teaspoons mustard seeds

1 teaspoon black peppercorns

1 teaspoon pink peppercorns

2 cups white wine vinegar

1 cup sherry vinegar

1½ cups water

3 tablespoons kosher salt

2 teaspoons sugar

STEM the tomatoes, then prick each one with a darning needle in a couple of places.

PEEL and halve or quarter the shallots lengthwise, leaving the stem ends intact. The pieces should be about the same size as garlic cloves. Peel the garlic cloves but leave them whole. Mix the bay leaves, coriander seeds, mustard seeds, and peppercorns together in a small bowl.

IN A NONREACTIVE SAUCEPAN, combine the white wine and sherry vinegars, the water, salt, and sugar in a saucepan. Bring to a boil.

ARRANGE in layers in clean, hot jars the tomatoes, shallots, garlic, and spice mixture, making sure to distribute the ingredients evenly among the jars. Pour the hot vinegar mixture into the jars, leaving a ¼-inch headspace. Slip a skewer or chopstick gently between the tomatoes and the side of each jar to release air bubbles. Process in a boiling water bath (see page 30) for 10 minutes for long-term storage. Or pack into sterilized jars, cover, and store in the refrigerator for up to 6 months. Allow to stand for at least 6 weeks, to mellow the flavors before opening or giving away.

pickled JALAPEÑOS

If you thought that pickled jalapeños are simply hot, think again. These are incredibly flavorful. They make a special gift for anyone who loves the heat of chiles.

1 head garlic

2 pounds fresh jalapeño chiles

2 or 3 sprigs oregano, or
    1 teaspoon dried oregano

2 or 3 sprigs thyme, or 1 teaspoon
    dried thyme

2 or 3 sprigs marjoram, or
    1 teaspoon dried marjoram

3 tablespoons olive oil

2 white onions, thickly sliced

4 carrots, peeled and thickly sliced

4 teaspoons kosher salt

$1/2$ teaspoon coarsely ground black
    pepper

2 bay leaves

5 cups distilled white vinegar

$1/2$ cup water

SEPARATE the garlic cloves and peel them, but leave them whole. (For quick peeling, blanch the garlic cloves in boiling water for about 30 seconds.)

PICK over the chiles, discarding any with soft spots.

BREAK the oregano, thyme, and marjoram sprigs into 3- to 4-inch pieces and distribute them evenly among clean (or sterilized, if not processing in a boiling water bath) pint jars. If using dried herbs, mix them together and sprinkle a generous pinch into the bottom of each jar.

IN A 6-QUART or larger nonreactive pot, heat the olive oil over medium heat. Add the garlic, onions, and carrots and stir for about 5 minutes, or until wilted but not browned. Add the jalapeños, salt, pepper, bay leaves, vinegar, and water. Increase the heat to high, bring to a boil, decrease the heat to medium, and simmer for 1 minute.

SET a colander over a bowl and ladle all of the vegetables into it, reserving the liquid in the pot and whatever collects in the bowl.

PACK the chiles and vegetables into the jars. Pour in the hot vinegar mixture, leaving a $1/4$-inch headspace. Gently slip a wooden skewer or chopstick between the chiles and the side of each jar to release air bubbles. Seal and process in a boiling water bath (see page 30) for 10 minutes for long-term storage. Or pack into sterilized jars, cover, and store in the refrigerator for up to 6 months. Allow to stand for at least 2 weeks to mellow the flavors before opening or giving away.

oven-dried **TOMATOES**

Deep, rich, and intense in flavor, these tomatoes are a great improvement over commercially dried tomatoes. The friend who loves to cook will find many uses for a jar of them, and the friend who doesn't cook will love to add them to a sandwich. Accompany your jar with a loaf of country bread, some goat cheese, and a bunch of basil to get them started. Choose pretty half-pint jars (they don't have to be canning jars) and tie them up with a deep red ribbon or piece of raffia.

You can use tomatoes from your garden, from your local farm stand, and out of season from your supermarket. I've suggested particular herbs and spices, but experiment using any seasoning you enjoy with tomatoes. Rosemary, oregano, sage, marjoram, and cumin seeds are all good choices. If you like a little heat, add some crushed red pepper flakes to the mix.

4 pounds plum tomatoes

1 teaspoon kosher salt

1 teaspoon coriander seeds

1 teaspoon dried thyme leaves

$1/2$ teaspoon sugar

$1/2$ teaspoon fennel seeds

$1/4$ teaspoon coarsely ground black pepper

1 teaspoon finely grated orange zest

Olive oil

PREHEAT the oven to 225°. Line a baking sheet with aluminum foil.

HALVE the tomatoes lengthwise. Working with a tomato half at a time, squeeze gently as you scrape out excess liquid and loose seeds with your finger. Arrange the tomatoes close together, cut sides up, on the prepared baking sheet. They will shrink considerably during the drying process.

COMBINE the salt, coriander seeds, thyme, sugar, fennel seeds, and pepper in a mortar and grind until the seeds are coarsely crushed and the ingredients are well mixed. Add the orange zest and mix well with your fingers. (If you don't have a mortar, crush the seeds with a rolling pin or a small, heavy skillet and mix all of the ingredients together in a bowl.)

(continued)

SPRINKLE the tomatoes evenly with the spice mixture. Bake the tomatoes for 4 to 6 hours, until they are dry but still slightly pliable. The time will vary depending on the size and thickness of the tomatoes. It can take up to 8 hours if the tomatoes are large or very juicy. Check after about $3^1/2$ hours and remove any that seem dry enough, then continue to bake the others. They will look a little like dried peaches when done. Allow to cool thoroughly.

PACK the tomatoes in sterilized jars and pour in enough olive oil to cover the tomatoes by about $^1/_4$ inch. Slip a skewer or chopstick between the tomatoes and the side of each jar to release air bubbles. Cover and store in the refrigerator. The tomatoes will keep refrigerated for up to 3 months, as long as they are submerged in oil. Before using, remove the jar from the refrigerator and allow it to come to room temperature so that the congealed oil can liquefy. The flavorful oil can be used in cooking.

preserved **LEMONS**

▶ MAKES 2 PINT JARS

A fellow cook would love a jar of preserved lemons, perhaps bundled with one of Paula Wolfert's excellent books on Mediterranean or Moroccan cooking. An attractive jar is part of the present and will need little adornment, unless you want to wrap it in bright yellow tissue tied with a leafy green ribbon. For the uninitiated, add a tag to suggest using these to flavor sauces, braised dishes, vegetable stews, roast chicken, fish, rice, or even tuna salad.

Purchase organic lemons, if possible. Sweet Meyer lemons, available for about a month in late winter, look nice in the jar but are not necessary. Substitute small thin-skinned lemons, since thick-skinned fruits take longer to soften. The flower cut is not mandatory either, but is a nice aesthetic touch.

8 or 9 small Meyer lemons, or 5 to 7 small regular lemons, plus a few additional lemons for juice

About $\frac{1}{2}$ cup kosher salt

2 bay leaves

2 2-inch-long cinnamon sticks

6 whole cloves

SCRUB the lemons. If they are not organic, immerse them in boiling water for 30 seconds to remove any pesticides and wax. Cool them in a bowl of ice water.

MAKE 2 deep vertical incisions in each lemon to divide it into quarters, but don't cut all the way through. You will have a lemon "flower." If the lemons are large, you may just want to quarter them and arrange them nicely in the jar after salting.

SPRINKLE 1 tablespoon of the salt in the bottom of each sterilized jar. Sprinkle the inside of each lemon "flower" with a rounded tablespoon of salt and pack into the jars. Press down as you pack the lemons to release some juice and to fit as many as you can into each jar. Wedge a bay leaf and cinnamon stick

(continued)

between the lemons and the side of the jars. Add the cloves. If needed, add additional lemon juice to cover the lemons. Seal the jars.

LET stand for 1 week at room temperature, inverting the jars occasionally to distribute the salt and juice. Then store the jars in the refrigerator for up to 6 months. When the rinds soften (about 2 weeks), the lemons are ready. To use, rinse the lemon, scrape away the pulp, and dice the rind. If white crystals appear, the lemons may still be used. Just rinse them first.

homemade grainy MUSTARD

▶ MAKES 3 HALF-PINT JARS

If you're feeling ambitious, give a jar of this mustard with one or two other homemade condiments, or just bag it up with some good rye bread, a hunk of cheese, and a six-pack of your favorite beer. It's hard to predict how hot a batch of this mustard will turn out, since it tastes a little different every time. While two kinds of mustard seeds aren't absolutely essential (brown ones can be hard to find), the two colors look interesting. You will wonder why you didn't make this before, it's so good and so easy to do.

3/4 cup yellow mustard seeds

1/4 cup brown mustard seeds

3 tablespoons honey

1/3 cup sherry or malt vinegar

1/4 cup Irish whiskey

1 tablespoon fine sea salt

COMBINE the yellow and brown mustard seeds in a bowl, cover with water, and leave to soak for 6 to 8 hours or as long as overnight.

DRAIN the seeds well and pour them into a food processor. Process until the mixture begins to look creamy and emulsified. Add the honey, vinegar, whiskey, and salt and process again to mix.

POUR the mustard into a bowl, cover, and let stand overnight at room temperature. The next day, check the consistency and flavor. If it is too thick and the taste is perfect, add a little more water. Adjust the other ingredients according to your taste. It will be hot!

SPOON the mustard into sterilized jars, cover, and store in the refrigerator, where it will keep almost indefinitely. Homemade mustard benefits from at least a week's rest before using to allow the flavors to blend.

red TOMATO and PEACH CHUTNEY

▶ MAKES ABOUT 4 PINT JARS

This deep amber chutney is the quintessence of summer's end. Give it with a loaf of whole-grain bread and a piece of sharp Cheddar, and save some for yourself for a delicious lunch on the run. Salting and draining the tomatoes in a colander to eliminate excess juice cuts down on the cooking time, which keeps the peaches from becoming too soft. As with most chutneys, it's best to store it for about 3 weeks before opening to allow the flavors to mellow.

CORE the tomatoes and halve them crosswise. Gently squeeze each half to remove the seeds. Cut into $^1/_2$-inch dice. Layer the tomatoes with the salt in a large colander set over a bowl and allow to drain for 2 hours.

BRING a 4-quart or larger pot of water to a boil. Halve each peach by cutting along the crease through to the pit. Twist the halves gently in opposite directions to release them from the pit, then remove the pit with a teaspoon. Working with 4 or 5 peaches at a time, drop the halves into the boiling water and blanch for 40 to 50 seconds to loosen the skins. Transfer them with a slotted spoon to a bowl of cold water for another 30 seconds to cool, then slip off the skins and slice thinly. You should have 6 to 7 cups.

IN A 6-QUART or larger nonreactive pot, combine the drained tomatoes, peaches, onion, raisins, ginger, jalapeños, and vinegar. Bring to a simmer over medium heat and simmer, uncovered, for 15 minutes, or until the vegetables are tender. Add the brown sugar and continue to cook for 15 to 20 minutes longer, until thick, stirring occasionally.

2 $^1/_2$ pounds firm, ripe tomatoes

1 $^1/_2$ teaspoons kosher salt

2 $^1/_2$ pounds peaches

1 large onion, sliced
(about 2 cups)

$^3/_4$ cup golden raisins

$^1/_2$ cup julienned peeled gingerroot

2 jalapeño chiles, seeded and
finely chopped

1 $^1/_2$ cups distilled white vinegar

1 $^1/_4$ cups firmly packed light brown
sugar

(continued)

LADLE the hot chutney into clean, hot jars, leaving a $^1/_4$-inch headspace, seal, and process in a boiling water bath (see page 30) for 10 minutes for long-term storage. Or ladle into sterilized jars, cover, and store in the refrigerator for up to 6 months. Allow to sit for at least 3 weeks before opening or giving away.

GINGER

When shopping for gingerroot, look for shiny skin on fleshy roots. A dull and wrinkled exterior indicates that the ginger is probably old. Try peeling it with the edge of a teaspoon or melon baller to get around all the nooks and crannies.

POSTHOLIDAY SLUMP BUSTER

Fill a basket with jars of your home-made pickles, chutney, and mustard and a loaf of your favorite rye bread to go along with the holiday leftovers.

cranberry CHUTNEY

▶ MAKES ABOUT 4 PINT JARS

Since chutney is at its best if allowed to ripen for at least 3 weeks, I try to make a batch of this chutney as soon as cranberries appear in the market before the holidays. If you haven't planned ahead, it is still very good if you make it the night before Thanksgiving and bring it along to the family dinner.

1 large onion, halved and thinly sliced (about 2 cups)

2 cups water

1 cup granulated sugar

1$^1/_2$ cups firmly packed brown sugar

4 juice oranges

4 firm cooking apples, peeled, cored, and cut into $^1/_2$-inch dice (about 4 cups)

2-inch piece gingerroot, peeled and cut into 1-inch matchstick

2 teaspoons ground mace

$^1/_2$ teaspoon ground cloves

1$^1/_4$ cups cider vinegar

2 (12-ounce) packages fresh cranberries, picked over

1 cup dried currants

IN A LARGE, heavy-bottomed nonreactive saucepan, combine the onion, water, and granulated and brown sugars. Bring to a boil, stir, decrease the heat to low, and simmer uncovered for 20 minutes while you prepare the other ingredients.

SCRUB the oranges. Quarter them through the stem end, discard the seeds, and slice them as thinly as possible. Alternatively, slice the whole oranges crosswise into 1/8-inch-thick rounds, removing the seeds as you slice, and chop them into small pieces in a food processor with a series of pulses. Take care not to reduce them to a purée.

ADD the orange slices and their juice, apples, ginger, mace, cloves, and vinegar to the saucepan and continue to cook for another 20 minutes. Add the cranberries and currants to the pan and continue to simmer for an additional 10 to 15 minutes, until the mixture is thick.

LADLE the hot chutney into clean, hot jars, leaving a $^1/_4$-inch headspace, seal, and process in a boiling water bath (see page 30) for 10 minutes for long-term storage. Or ladle into sterilized jars, cover, and store in the refrigerator for up to 6 months. Allow to sit for at least 3 weeks before opening or giving away.

cakes

chapter seven

Celebrations for Every Season

Old-fashioned homemade butter cakes are almost an endangered species, now relegated to once-a-year birthday celebrations. More often they come from bakeries, not someone's kitchen, and are slathered with overly sweet icing made from mysterious substances. That's what makes a simple cake such a pleasure to receive from a friend. Without an important occasion to mark, a slice of cake with a cup of tea suggests that we can and should commemorate the everyday and the pleasure of one another's company. Of course, a weekend hostess, your fellow office workers, or the family with eager little mouths to feed would be only too glad to accept your beautifully wrapped cake. For a special gift, add a box of imported tea or cocoa, a teapot, or a pretty antique plate.

The cakes in this chapter are loaf or Bundt cakes that are packed with flavor and in no need of icing. They are also quick to put together, keep well, and do not tax the gift giver with complicated techniques. These are the kind of cakes that would make your grandmother proud.

Disposable loaf pans (8 by $3^3/4$ by $2^1/2$-inch) are readily available at the supermarket and produce the perfect size cake for gift giving. Be sure to set them on a baking sheet to keep them steady in the oven. The pans themselves are not particularly elegant, so I recommend removing the cakes and cooling them on a rack before wrapping. Small Bundt or kuglehopf pans ($6^{1}/_{2}$-inch) also make pretty cakes and are a practical size for a gift.

Wrap loaf cakes in plastic and then cellophane. Tape them on the bottom with clear packing tape, which doesn't show, and tie them up with a big bow. Add a tag or a pretty ornament to embellish the ribbon. Place a Bundt cake on a pretty plate from the secondhand store, on a doily-lined cardboard circle, or on a festive paper plate. Place the cake and plate on a large piece of cellophane, gather the corners up to the middle, and tie with a ribbon.

STORING BUTTER CAKES

Butter cakes are best stored at room temperature and will stay fresh for 2 to 4 days wrapped in aluminum foil or plastic wrap. They can be frozen for 3 months if double-wrapped in foil and then slipped into a heavy plastic bag. Thaw the cakes at room temperature, and then, for the best results, place them in a 350° oven for 10 to 15 minutes to revive them.

apple-ginger CAKES

▶ MAKES 2 SMALL TUBE CAKES

Who can resist a slice of gingerbread served with a dollop of whipped cream? Grated apples and walnut oil help keep this classic cake from drying out after a day, making it ideal for gift giving, as well as for having around for a spur-of-the-moment tea party.

PREHEAT the oven to 350°. Butter and flour two 6 1/2-inch kugelhopf pans.

SIFT together the flour, baking powder, salt, and baking soda onto a piece of waxed paper. Combine the butter and sugar in a bowl. With a wooden spoon or an electric mixer on medium-high speed, beat for 3 to 4 minutes, until fluffy and light. Add the eggs one at a time, beating for about 30 seconds after each addition and scraping down the bowl as necessary. Add the oil, molasses, grated ginger, coriander, ground ginger, cloves, and cinnamon. Beat for 2 minutes on medium speed.

ADD the flour mixture to the batter in 2 batches, alternating with the coffee. Mix until well combined. Stir in the walnuts and apples. Spoon the batter into the prepared pans and smooth the tops with the back of a spoon.

BAKE for 35 to 40 minutes, until a toothpick inserted into the center of a cake comes out clean. Remove from the oven, let cool in the pans on a rack for 5 minutes, then turn the cakes out onto the rack to cool.

WRAPPED in plastic or aluminum foil, the cakes will keep for 2 to 3 days at room temperature and for up to 3 months in the freezer.

2 1/2 cups unbleached all-purpose flour

1 1/2 teaspoons baking powder

1 teaspoon salt

1/2 teaspoon baking soda

1/2 cup (1 stick) unsalted butter, at room temperature

1/2 cup sugar

3 eggs

1/3 cup walnut or mild vegetable oil

1 cup dark molasses

1 tablespoon peeled, finely grated fresh ginger

1 tablespoon ground coriander

1 teaspoon ground ginger

1 teaspoon ground cloves

1 teaspoon ground cinnamon

1/2 cup strong brewed coffee, at room temperature

1 cup coarsely chopped walnuts

1 large tart apple, peeled, cored, and coarsely grated (about 1 cup)

lavender-lemon TEA CAKES

▶ MAKES 2 LOAF CAKES

Lavender flowers are decidedly old-fashioned, as is this not-too-rich tea loaf. You can usually find the flowers in a health food store that sells herbs and spices in bulk. Wrap the cakes in cellophane, tie them with purple ribbon, and attach a yellow lemon-shaped tag to the package.

Grinding the almonds in a food processor with a little of the sugar will keep them from turning into nut butter. Use blanched whole almonds or whole almonds with their natural brown skins, depending on the effect you want. Ground unblanched almonds give the cake a homey look, while blanched almonds are less noticeable, emphasizing the flecks of lavender.

3 cups unbleached all-purpose
   flour

1 tablespoon baking powder

1 teaspoon salt

$^3/_4$ cup almonds

$1^1/_2$ cups sugar

Finely grated zest and juice of
   2 lemons ($^1/_3$ to $^1/_2$ cup juice)

$^1/_2$ cup (1 stick) unsalted butter,
   at room temperature

6 eggs, at room temperature

$^1/_2$ cup buttermilk

2 tablespoons dried lavender
   flowers

PREHEAT the oven to 350°. Butter and flour two 8 by $3^3/_4$ by $2^1/_2$-inch disposable aluminum loaf pans.

SIFT together the flour, baking powder, and salt onto a piece of waxed paper. Set aside.

IN A FOOD PROCESSOR, grind the almonds with 2 tablespoons of the sugar. Set aside.

COMBINE the remaining sugar and the lemon zest in a mixing bowl. With your hands, rub the lemon zest into the sugar. Add the butter. With a wooden spoon or electric mixer set on medium-high speed, beat for about 3 minutes, or until very light and fluffy. Add the eggs one at a time, beating for about 30 seconds after each addition and scraping down the sides of the bowl as necessary. Beat in the lemon juice.

(continued)

ADD half of the flour and beat in on low speed. Add all of the buttermilk, and then the remaining flour, beating on low speed after each addition just until the ingredients are blended. Finally, add the ground almonds and lavender flowers, again mixing just until combined. Spoon the batter into the prepared pans and smooth the tops with the back of a spoon.

BAKE for 55 to 60 minutes, until the top is golden brown and a toothpick inserted into the center of a loaf comes out clean. Remove from the oven, let cool in the pans on a rack for 10 minutes, then turn the cakes out onto the rack to cool.

WRAPPED in plastic or aluminum foil, the cakes will keep for 2 to 3 days at room temperature and for up to 3 months in the freezer.

► MAKES 2 LOAF CAKES

Remember cream cheese on date-nut bread? Here's a pleasant change that your grand-mother or aunt might enjoy, with or without the cream cheese. Wrap the cake neatly in plastic and then in cellophane, tape it at the bottom with clear packing tape, and tie it with a chocolate-colored satin ribbon.

The date-nut combination still rings true, but you can experiment with other dried fruits like cherries, cranberries, pears, or apricots.

PREHEAT the oven to 350°. Butter and flour two 8 by $3^3/_4$ by $2^1/_2$-inch disposable aluminum loaf pans.

SIFT together the flour, cocoa, baking powder, baking soda, and salt onto a piece of waxed paper. Set aside.

COMBINE the sugar and butter in a mixing bowl. With a wooden spoon or an electric mixer set on medium-high speed, beat for 3 to 5 minutes, until very light and fluffy. Add the eggs one at a time, beating for about 30 seconds after each addition and scraping down the sides of the bowl as necessary. Add the orange zest and brandy and beat for 1 more minute.

ADD the flour mixture in 3 batches alternately with the buttermilk, beginning and ending with flour, and beat on low speed after each addition, just until the ingredients are blended. Stir in the walnuts and dates. Spoon the batter into the prepared pans and smooth the tops with the back of a spoon.

BAKE for 55 to 60 minutes, until a toothpick inserted into the center of a loaf comes out clean. Remove from the oven and let cool in the pans on a rack for 10 minutes, then turn out of the pans onto the rack to cool.

WRAPPED in plastic or aluminum foil, the cakes will keep for 2 to 3 days at room temperature and up to 3 months in the freezer.

$1^3/_4$ cups unbleached all-purpose flour

$^1/_3$ cup Dutch-process cocoa powder

$^1/_2$ teaspoon baking powder

$^1/_2$ teaspoon baking soda

$^1/_2$ teaspoon salt

$1^1/_3$ cups sugar

1 cup (2 sticks) unsalted butter, at room temperature

4 eggs

Finely grated zest of 1 orange

2 tablespoons orange-flavored brandy

$^2/_3$ cup buttermilk

1 cup coarsely chopped walnut pieces

1 cup dates, cut into $^1/_4$-inch pieces

double espresso BANANA-WALNUT CAKES

▶ MAKES 2 SMALL TUBE CAKES

Here's a banana bread with a deep espresso flavor—for grown-ups. A package of your favorite coffee beans would complement this gift nicely. If the occasion calls for it, the recipe will make a single large tube cake. Use a 9 1/2-inch pan and bake the cake for 50 to 60 minutes.

PREHEAT the oven to 350°. Butter and flour two 6 1/2-inch kugelhopf pans.

Place the bananas in a bowl and mash with a potato masher or with an electric mixer. Set aside.

SIFT together the all-purpose and whole-wheat flours, baking powder, baking soda, and salt onto a piece of waxed paper. Set aside.

COMBINE the butter and brown sugar in a mixing bowl. With a wooden spoon or an electric mixer set on medium-high speed, beat for 3 to 5 minutes, until very light and fluffy. Add the eggs one at a time, beating for about 30 seconds after each addition and scraping down the sides of the bowl as necessary. Add the oil, vanilla, dissolved espresso powder, yogurt, and mashed bananas and beat on medium speed until smooth.

ADD the dry flour mixture and beat on low speed just until blended. Stir in the walnuts. Spoon the batter into the prepared pans and smooth the tops with the back of a spoon.

BAKE for about 40 minutes, or until a toothpick inserted into the center of a cake comes out clean. Remove from the oven and let rest in the pans on a rack for 10 minutes, then turn out of the pans onto the rack to cool.

WRAPPED in plastic or aluminum foil, the cakes will keep for 2 to 3 days at room temperature and for up to 3 months in the freezer.

1 pound ripe bananas (3 to 4), peeled

1 cup unbleached all-purpose flour

3/4 cup whole-wheat flour

1 1/2 teaspoons baking powder

1/2 teaspoon baking soda

1/2 teaspoon salt

1/4 cup (1/2 stick) unsalted butter, at room temperature

3/4 cup firmly packed brown sugar

2 eggs

1/4 cup walnut oil

1 teaspoon vanilla extract

1 heaping teaspoon instant espresso powder dissolved in 1 tablespoon boiling water

1/2 cup plain yogurt

1/2 cup coarsely chopped walnuts

hazelnut LOAF CAKES

▶ MAKES 2 LOAF CAKES

Hazelnut oil, toasted nuts, and liqueur might seem like overkill, but the trio gives this moist cake a deep hazelnut essence. This one's a winner for your friend with a sweet tooth and a penchant for afternoon coffee.

1¼ cups hazelnuts

2¼ cups unbleached all-purpose flour

½ teaspoon baking powder

½ teaspoon baking soda

¾ teaspoon salt

1¼ cups sugar

½ cup (1 stick) unsalted butter, at room temperature

4 eggs

⅓ cup toasted hazelnut oil

Finely grated zest of 1 orange

1 teaspoon vanilla extract

3 tablespoons Frangelico (hazelnut liqueur)

¾ cup sour cream

PREHEAT the oven to 350°. Butter and flour two 8 by 3¾ by 2½-inch disposable aluminum loaf pans.

SPREAD the hazelnuts on a baking sheet and toast in the oven for 15 to 20 minutes, until the skins crack and pull away from the nuts. While still hot, wrap them in a slightly damp towel (terry cloth works best) and rub to remove the skins. Do not worry if tiny specks of skin remain. Let the nuts cool.

BY HAND or in a food processor, chop the nuts fairly finely. You want them to have a little texture but not be too large. Spread them on the baking sheet again and return them to the oven for 10 to 15 minutes, until brown and very toasty.

SIFT together the flour, baking powder, baking soda, and salt onto a piece of waxed paper. Set aside.

COMBINE the sugar and butter in a mixing bowl. With a wooden spoon or an electric mixer set on medium-high speed, beat for 3 to 5 minutes, until very light and fluffy. Add the eggs one at a time, beating for about 30 seconds after each addition and scraping down the sides of the bowl as necessary. Add the oil, orange zest, vanilla, and Frangelico and beat for 1 more minute.

ADD half of the flour mixture, all of the sour cream, and then the remaining flour mixture, beating on low speed after each addition, just until the ingredients are blended. Set aside 2 tablespoons of the hazelnuts and stir the rest of the nuts into the batter. Spoon the batter into prepared pans and smooth the tops with the back of a spoon. Sprinkle the reserved nuts in a line down the center of the top of each loaf.

BAKE for 50 to 60 minutes, until a toothpick inserted into the center of a loaf comes out clean. Remove from the oven and let cool in the pans on a rack for 10 minutes, then turn out of the pans onto the rack to cool.

WRAPPED in plastic or aluminum foil, the cakes will keep for 2 to 3 days at room temperature and for up to 3 months in the freezer.

BETTER CAKES

Take plenty of time to beat the butter and sugar together until fluffy and pale. As you beat, the butter becomes aerated and forms little bubbles. The leavening, usually baking powder, will then expand these bubbles when the cake bakes, resulting in a light and tender crumb.

NONSTICK CAKES

Prepare cake pans by buttering them and then dusting them with flour. Sprinkle the flour over the buttered pan, tilt and shake the pan to distribute it evenly, and tap out the excess. As an extra precaution, line the bottom of the buttered and floured pan with a piece of parchment paper.

TO TEST FOR DONENESS

Insert a toothpick into the center of the cake to test for doneness. It should come out clean, without a trace of batter. Another sign: The cake will shrink a little and start to pull away from the sides of the pan. Test a few minutes before the prescribed time and often after that. Once out of the oven, let the cake rest for 5 to 10 minutes in the pan on a rack, to allow it to firm up a little before turning it out onto the rack to cool.

cookies

chapter eight

The Home Bakery

When I was a child, in our house Christmas cookies meant only one thing: rolled cookies cut into shapes and sprinkled with homemade colored sugar. We children made a colossal mess, ate half of the dough, and presented our efforts to our parents, who hid out in the living room away from the chaos. I still have some of those cookie cutters and enjoy watching my son cut out his favorite gingerbread Santas, stars, and farm animals.

Because cookies are so easy to make, they're the obvious gift for holiday giving. But don't forget about them during the rest of the year. A tin of home-made cookies taken on a picnic or to a friend in distress can go a long way toward making the company just a bit merrier.

Wrapping cookies for gifts can be a simple affair. A tin from the cookware store or five-and-ten, a colored paper plate wrapped in clear cellophane and tied with a special ribbon, or a kid-inspired cellophane bag from a party supply store will do the job nicely. Consider, too, collecting odd plates, bowls, or jars from flea markets to use as containers. One of my best surprise finds was to discover large (and cheap) honey jars at a local artist supply store. Keep an eye out for these things all year long and stash them away until the occasion calls for them.

If cookies are fairly sturdy and of uniform size, you can stack them, roll them up in a flat piece of clear cellophane to form a tube, tape the sides

DECORATING ROLLED COOKIES

Decorating cookies around the holidays can be fun for the whole family. You can simply sprinkle cookies with colored sugar (mix food coloring with granulated sugar for homemade colored sugar) or colored jimmies (sprinkles) from the cake section of the supermarket before baking, or you can decorate more elaborately with icing. The icing can be further dressed up with a sprinkling of colored stuff before it sets. Here are a couple of icing ideas.

ROYAL ICING

In a bowl, combine 1 egg white with 1 cup confectioners' sugar and mix with a spoon until smooth. If desired, tint with food coloring. Pipe or spread onto cooled cookies. Let the icing dry thoroughly (it becomes hard) before storing the cookies between sheets of waxed paper. If raw egg whites make you nervous, use meringue powder. Adjust the consistency to your liking by adding more confectioners' sugar or a few drops of water.

(continued on page 108)

together with clear packing tape that doesn't show, and tie the cylinder together with ribbon at each end. Use shiny foil wrapping paper if it is a holiday gift, or for a homespun look, wrap the cylinder in brown paper (lined with a piece of cellophane or plastic wrap to keep it free of grease spots) and tie with a piece of string or raffia.

An assortment of small cookies on a pretty plate makes an ideal holiday gift. Make a pyramid of cookies on the plate (or on a doily-lined cardboard cake circle), enclose it in cellophane, gather the top, and tie with a ribbon. You could also divide the cookie varieties among white muffin-cup liners and arrange them on the plate. Gift boxes or white cardboard candy boxes lined with tissue and waxed paper can also be packed this way. Children love to receive their own special stash of cookies in a small box with their name on it. For a fellow baker, pack the cookies in a ceramic baking dish or metal baking pan to create a gift that can be enjoyed over and over again.

all-purpose SUGAR COOKIES

► MAKES ABOUT 6 DOZEN 3-INCH COOKIES

These basic cookies are essential to every holiday—the cookies that you remember from childhood and that your children will remember, too. Don't forget autumn leaves, Halloween pumpkins and bats, Easter ducks, and spring umbrellas. Kids' favorite shapes, such as teapots for a teddy bear party or airplanes and cars for your son's birthday, will delight all the little folks on your list.

For variation, add $^1/_2$ teaspoon lemon extract and the finely grated zest of a lemon to the dough.

1 cup (2 sticks) unsalted butter, at room temperature

1$^1/_2$ cups sugar

2 eggs

1$^1/_2$ teaspoons vanilla extract

3$^1/_2$ cups unbleached all-purpose flour

1 teaspoon baking powder

$^1/_2$ teaspoon salt

Royal Icing (page 106) or White Chocolate Icing (page 108) (optional)

COMBINE the butter with the sugar in a mixing bowl. With a wooden spoon or an electric mixer set on medium speed, beat until light and creamy. Add the eggs and vanilla and mix just until blended.

SIFT together the flour, baking powder, and salt onto a piece of waxed paper. Gradually add it to the butter mixture, stirring only enough to combine all the ingredients evenly.

SCRAPE the dough onto a large piece of plastic wrap. Pat it into a flat rectangle, enclose it in the plastic, and refrigerate for about 1 hour, or until firm.

PREHEAT the oven to 350°. Lightly butter baking sheets or line with parchment paper.

WORKING with about one-quarter of the dough at a time, roll the dough out on a lightly floured surface to a thickness of $^1/_8$ inch. Using cookie cutters, cut out shapes and transfer them to the prepared baking sheets, spacing them about 1 inch apart. Gather the dough scraps and incorporate the scraps into the

(continued)

WHITE CHOCOLATE ICING

Melt white chocolate and pipe or spread on completely cooled cookies. Be aware that not all white chocolates are created equal, and some (namely, white chocolate morsels from the supermarket) don't always contain enough cocoa butter to flow through a squeeze bottle when melted. If necessary, thin with a teaspoon or so of mild vegetable oil. (Never use water, or the chocolate will seize.) If you want to tint white chocolate, use very small amounts of paste food coloring (from a cake-decorating supply store). Ordinary liquid food coloring will cause melted chocolate to seize. Leave the decorated cookies in a cool place until the chocolate hardens before storing between sheets of waxed paper. You can use dark or milk chocolate in the same way.

THE SQUEEZE BOTTLE

Chefs on television use squeeze bottles to decorate fancy plated desserts with swirls of chocolate or raspberry, but they're also a boon to cookie decorators. Kids (and many adults) have a much easier time squeezing out Royal Icing or melted chocolate from a squeeze bottle than a pastry bag. Look for them in cake-decorating supply stores or cookware catalogs.

second piece of dough. Roll out and cut as before. Continue gathering scraps and rolling and cutting until all the dough is used.

BAKE the cookies for 12 to 16 minutes, until they are light brown on the bottom. Carefully transfer to wire racks to cool.

DECORATE with icing. The cookies will keep for about 2 weeks in a tightly closed tin. (If the cookies are decorated, separate the layers with waxed paper.)

GINGERBREAD cutouts

Kids love to make and give these cookies. And why not? They're fun to roll and cut into oh-so-many shapes. A few decorated cookies wrapped in a small cellophane bag and tied with ribbon makes a great birthday party favor. Cut the dough into shapes that correspond to the party's theme.

The Sucanat (granulated dried cane juice, available at natural food stores) has a less jolting effect than refined sugar and gives the cookies "freckles," little brown dots of undissolved sugar crystals. If you can't find it, brown sugar can be substituted.

The recipe can be doubled and the extra dough will keep tightly sealed in plastic wrap for 1 week in the refrigerator. The dough can also be frozen for up to 6 months.

COMBINE the butter and Sucanat in a mixing bowl. Using a wooden spoon or an electric mixer set on medium-high speed, beat until smooth. Stir in the egg and molasses. The mixture may look curdled, but it will smooth out when you add the flour.

SIFT together the flour, ginger, cinnamon, cloves, nutmeg, baking soda, and salt onto a piece of waxed paper. Add to the butter and molasses mixture, stirring just until all the ingredients are evenly mixed.

SCRAPE the dough onto a large piece of plastic wrap. Pat it into a thick rectangle and enclose it in the plastic. Refrigerate for about 1 hour, or until firm.

PREHEAT the oven to 350°. Lightly butter baking sheets or line with parchment.

(continued)

$^1/_2$ cup unsalted butter (1 stick), at room temperature

$^1/_2$ cup Sucanat or firmly packed light or dark brown sugar

1 egg

$^1/_2$ cup dark molasses

2$^1/_2$ cups unbleached all-purpose flour

2 teaspoons ground ginger

2 teaspoons ground cinnamon

$^1/_2$ teaspoon ground cloves

$^1/_2$ teaspoon ground nutmeg

$^1/_2$ teaspoon baking soda

$^1/_2$ teaspoon salt

Royal Icing (page 106) or White Chocolate Icing (page 108) (optional)

Before baking, poke a hole in the top
of each cookie with the narrow end of
a chopstick or a plastic drinking
straw. When the cookies are cool and
decorated, use ribbon to tie a loop
through the hole.

ROLL out half the dough on a lightly floured surface to a thickness of $^1/_8$ inch. Using cookie cutters, cut out shapes and transfer them to the prepared baking sheets, spacing them about 1 inch apart. Gather the dough scraps and incorporate them into the remaining dough. Roll out and cut out as before until all the dough is used.

BAKE the cookies for 12 to 15 minutes, until they are light brown on the bottom. Carefully transfer to wire racks to cool.

DECORATE with icing. The cookies will keep for about 2 weeks in a tightly closed tin. (If the cookies are decorated, separate the layers with waxed paper.)

PALETS de dames

These traditional French cookies are crisp, shiny, and buttery without being overly rich. A little different from standard American fare, they are elegant alone with tea or presented as part of an assortment of small cookies. Tuck a dainty teacup and a tin of your favorite tea into your gift package to make it special.

1 cup whole unblanched almonds

³/₄ cup sugar

10 tablespoons (5 ounces) unsalted butter, at room temperature, cut into 1-inch pieces

2 eggs

1 teaspoon vanilla extract

1¹/₃ cups unbleached all-purpose flour

1 cup dried currants

2 teaspoons water

COMBINE the almonds and sugar in a food processor and process until the nuts are finely ground. Add the butter pieces, 1 egg, and the vanilla. Pulse just until combined. Add the flour and pulse briefly to blend.

SCRAPE the dough into a bowl and stir in the currants by hand. Then scrape the dough onto a large piece of plastic wrap. Pat it into a flat rectangle, enclose it in the plastic, and refrigerate for about 1 hour, or until firm.

PREHEAT the oven to 350°. Lightly butter baking sheets or line with parchment paper. In a small dish, beat the remaining egg thoroughly with the water.

ROLL out half the dough on a lightly floured surface to a thickness of ¹/₈ inch. Using a fluted 2-inch-round cookie cutter, cut out rounds and transfer them to the prepared baking sheets, spacing them 1 inch apart. Gather the dough scraps and incorporate them into the remaining dough. Roll it out as before until all the dough is used. Brush the tops of the cookies with the egg glaze.

BAKE the cookies for 15 to 18 minutes, until the tops are golden brown. Carefully transfer to a rack to cool. The cookies will keep for about 1 week in a tightly closed tin.

hazelnut SHORTBREAD

▶ MAKES ABOUT 4 DOZEN COOKIES

I can't have these around the house: they're simply too tempting. They must be wrapped and given away ASAP. You can make them in rounds or in the traditional thick rectangles (see variation). Other nuts, especially pecans and walnuts, are good to use in place of the hazelnuts. Toast them in a 350° oven for about 10 minutes to accentuate their fragrance.

(pictured, page 120)

3/4 cup hazelnuts

1 cup (2 sticks) unsalted butter, at room temperature

1/2 cup lightly packed brown sugar

2 tablespoons Frangelico (hazelnut liqueur) or brandy

1 teaspoon vanilla extract

2 cups unbleached all-purpose flour

Scant 1/4 teaspoon salt

PREHEAT the oven to 350°.

SPREAD the hazelnuts on a baking sheet and toast in the oven for 15 to 20 minutes, until the skins crack and pull away from the nuts. While still hot, wrap them in a towel (slightly damp terry cloth works best) and rub to remove the skins. Do not worry if tiny specks of skin remain. Let cool, then finely chop them with a knife or in a food processor.

BEAT the butter with a wooden spoon or an electric mixer set on medium speed for about 30 seconds, or until creamy. Add the sugar and beat until blended. Scrape down the sides of the bowl and beat in the liqueur and vanilla.

SIFT together the flour and salt onto a piece of waxed paper. Add the flour mixture to the creamed butter, 1 cup at a time, beating on low speed after each addition just until the flour is incorporated. Add the nuts and mix briefly until smooth.

SCRAPE the dough onto a large piece of plastic wrap. Pat it into a thick rectangle, enclose it in the plastic, and refrigerate for about 1 hour, or until firm.

PREHEAT the oven to 325°. Lightly butter baking sheets or line them with parchment paper.

(continued)

Holiday baking is a snap with a roll or two of icebox cookies in the refrigerator or freezer. The shaped dough will keep for a week or so in the refrigerator, and may be frozen (double wrap it) for up to 6 months. There is no need to thaw the dough. Just slice and bake frozen, as directed in the recipe, adding a few minutes to the baking time.

ROLL out half the dough on a lightly floured surface to a thickness of $1/4$ inch. Using a fluted 2-inch round cookie cutter, cut out rounds and transfer them to the prepared baking sheets, spacing them about 1 inch apart. Gather the scraps of dough and incorporate them into the remaining dough. Roll and cut out as before until all the dough is used. Prick each cookie 3 times with the tines of a fork. Place the baking sheets in the refrigerator to chill for 30 minutes.

BAKE the cookies for 20 to 25 minutes, or until golden brown. Carefully transfer to a rack to cool. The cookies will keep for 3 to 4 weeks in a tightly closed tin.

Hazelnut Shortbread Rectangles

If you want to make traditional shortbread rectangles, cut out a 9 by 16-inch piece of parchment or waxed paper to fit in a 9 by 13-inch baking pan. Fit it in the pan, creasing it at the narrow ends. It should reach to the rim of the pan at the ends.

After mixing, turn the soft dough into the prepared pan, pat it out evenly, smooth the top, and press it snugly into the corners of the pan. With the back of a fork or a cake decorator's comb, draw decorative "stripes" along the length of the dough. Cover with plastic wrap and refrigerate for about 2 hours, or until firm.

Using the edges of the paper as handles, remove the chilled dough from the pan and set it on a flat surface. With a ruler as a guide, cut the sheet into 1 by 2-inch rectangles. Place the rectangles 1 inch apart on buttered or parchment-lined baking sheets. Bake in the preheated 325° oven for 25 to 35 minutes, until golden. Cool and store as for the round shortbread cookies.

auntie rose's ICEBOX COOKIES

▶ MAKES ABOUT 9 DOZEN SMALL COOKIES

Everyone in my family looked forward to packages of my grandmother's tiny cookies at Christmas, which always included these icebox gems, made from her sister Rose's recipe. They were and are the hands-down favorites. Christmas just isn't Christmas without them. Try them once and you'll never make less than a double batch.

1 cup (2 sticks) unsalted butter, at room temperature

1 cup firmly packed brown sugar

1 egg

1 teaspoon vanilla extract

2 cups unbleached all-purpose flour

$^1/_2$ teaspoon baking powder

$^1/_2$ teaspoon salt

1 cup chopped walnuts

COMBINE the butter and sugar in a mixing bowl. With a wooden spoon or an electric mixer set on medium speed, beat until creamy. Beat in the egg and vanilla, mixing until smooth.

SIFT together the flour, baking powder, and salt onto a piece of waxed paper. Add to the butter mixture and stir until blended. Stir in the walnuts.

SPREAD an 18-inch-long piece of plastic wrap on the countertop and spoon about one third of the dough onto it. With your hands, shape it into a log about 12 inches long and $1^1/_4$ inches in diameter. Encase the dough in the plastic wrap and roll it back and forth a few times to make a round, even roll. Twist the ends to close them. Divide the remaining dough in half and shape into logs the same way. Place the 3 logs on a flat tray for at least 4 hours, or until firm, or as long as overnight.

PREHEAT the oven to 350°. Lightly butter baking sheets or line with parchment paper.

SLICE the logs into $^1/_4$-inch-thick rounds and place them 1 inch apart on the prepared baking sheets. Bake the cookies for 15 to 18 minutes, until they are golden brown. Carefully transfer to a rack to cool. The cookies will keep for at least 2 weeks in a tightly closed tin.

pinwheel COOKIES

(pictured, page 120)

▶ MAKES ABOUT 9 DOZEN COOKIES

These old-fashioned vanilla-and-chocolate cookies definitely hit a nostalgic nerve. For an updated version, add a dash of orange zest.

2 ounces unsweetened chocolate, chopped

1¹/₂ cups (3 sticks) unsalted butter

1¹/₄ cups sugar

1 egg

1 teaspoon vanilla extract

3¹/₂ cups unbleached all-purpose flour

³/₄ teaspoon baking powder

³/₄ teaspoon salt

Finely grated zest of 1 large orange (about 1 tablespoon) (optional)

PLACE the chocolate in a heatproof bowl and place over hot water until melted. Stir until smooth and set aside to cool.

WITH A WOODEN SPOON or an electric mixer set on medium speed, beat the butter until creamy. Add the sugar and beat until smooth. Beat in the egg and vanilla until blended.

SIFT together the flour, baking powder, and salt onto a piece of waxed paper. Add to the butter mixture and stir just until blended.

DIVIDE the dough in half. Add the orange zest to half of the dough and mix well. Add the melted chocolate to the other half and mix well.

DIVIDE each portion of dough in half again and shape the quarter-portions into flat rectangles. Place a rectangle between 2 pieces of plastic wrap and roll out into a 6 by 12-inch rectangle. Repeat with the other 3 portions.

PLACE 1 rectangle of the light-colored dough on a work surface and peel off the top piece of plastic wrap. Set a rectangle of chocolate dough next to it, peel off the top piece of plastic, and flip the chocolate dough over onto the light dough. Peel off the top layer of plastic. With the help of the plastic on the bottom, roll up the 2 rectangles of dough together into a 12-inch-long cylinder. Repeat with remaining 2 rectangles of dough. Place the logs on a tray and refrigerate for at least 4 hours, or until firm, or as long as overnight.

PREHEAT the oven to 350°. Lightly butter baking sheets or line with parchment paper. Slice the logs into $1/4$-inch-thick rounds and set 1 inch apart on the prepared baking sheets.

BAKE the cookies for 10 to 12 minutes, until they are lightly browned on the bottom. Carefully transfer to racks to cool. The cookies will keep for at least 2 weeks in a tightly closed tin.

ginger PENNIES

▶ MAKES ABOUT 12 DOZEN SMALL COOKIES

These are perfect for giving in winter, to enjoy with tea on a snowy day. But they are also a wonderful summertime gift, delivered along with a jug of freshly squeezed lemonade to a heat-weary friend. If you like larger cookies, make your rolls thicker.

1 cup (2 sticks) unsalted butter, at room temperature

1 cup firmly packed dark brown sugar

$^1/_3$ cup dark molasses

1 egg

1 teaspoon vanilla extract

Finely grated zest of 1 lemon

3 cups unbleached all-purpose flour

2 tablespoons ground ginger

1 teaspoon ground cloves

1 teaspoon baking soda

$^1/_2$ teaspoon salt

About $^1/_3$ cup granulated sugar

COMBINE the butter and brown sugar in a mixing bowl. With a wooden spoon or an electric mixer set on medium speed, beat until smooth. Stir in the molasses, egg, vanilla, and lemon zest and mix until well combined.

SIFT together the flour, ginger, cloves, baking soda, and salt onto a piece of waxed paper. Add to the butter mixture and stir just until all of the ingredients are evenly mixed.

SPREAD an 18-inch-long piece of plastic wrap on a countertop and spoon about one third of the dough onto it. With your hands, shape it into a log about 12 inches long and $1^1/_4$ inches in diameter. Encase the dough in the plastic wrap and roll it back and forth a few times to make an evenly round roll. Twist the ends to close them. Divide the remaining dough in half and shape into logs the same way. Place the 3 logs on a flat tray in the refrigerator and chill for about 4 hours, or until firm, or as long as overnight.

PREHEAT the oven to 350°. Lightly butter baking sheets or line with parchment paper. Pour the granulated sugar into a saucer. Slice the logs into $^1/_4$-inch-thick rounds and dip them in the sugar, coating evenly. Set the cookies 1 inch apart on the prepared baking sheets.

BAKE the cookies for 10 to 12 minutes, until they are golden brown on the bottom. Carefully transfer to a rack to cool. The cookies will keep for at least 2 weeks in a tightly closed tin.

dainty SUGAR COOKIES

▶ MAKES ABOUT 10 DOZEN SMALL COOKIES

These are plain cookies (as in not too rich) with shiny tops. I'm not overly fond of glacéed cherries, but I confess that they add a nicely festive accent to a cookie assortment. You could substitute small walnut pieces, almonds, pecans, pine nuts, dried cherries, or dried cranberries, or you can make some of each.

(pictured, page 120)

PREHEAT the oven to 350°. Lightly butter baking sheets or line with parchment paper.

COMBINE the butter and sugar in a mixing bowl. With a wooden spoon or an electric mixer set on medium speed, beat until creamy. Add the egg yolks and vanilla and beat until smooth.

SIFT together the flour, baking powder, baking soda, and salt onto a piece of waxed paper. Add to the butter mixture and stir just until all of the ingredients are evenly mixed.

ROLL the dough into balls slightly smaller than 1 inch in diameter and place them 2 inches apart on the prepared baking sheets.

BRUSH the tops of the cookies with the egg white glaze. Press a piece of glacéed cherry into the top of each cookie. (Since the cookies are tiny, I usually cut the cherries into fourths.)

BAKE the cookies for 15 to 18 minutes, until they are a delicate brown. Carefully transfer to racks to cool. The cookies will keep for about 3 weeks in a tightly closed tin.

1 cup (2 sticks) unsalted butter, at room temperature

2 cups sugar

4 egg yolks

1 1/2 teaspoons vanilla extract

3 cups unbleached all-purpose flour

2 teaspoons baking powder

1/4 teaspoon baking soda

1/2 teaspoon salt

1 egg white beaten with 1 tablespoon water

1/4 pound glacéed cherries, halved or quartered

chocolate-apricot RUGELACH

(pictured, page 120)

▶ MAKES 6 DOZEN

I first made acquaintance with these irresistible cookies when I lived in Indiana. Whenever I went "back East" for a visit, a former New Yorker would send me on a mission to the Babka Bakery on the Upper West Side of Manhattan. My assignment was to procure a box of rugelach. Like all good things, the bakery has come to an end, but the cookies are accessible without the trip. Shaping the dough in flat rounds before chilling makes rolling much easier. Use parchment paper to line the pans for painless cleanup.

TO MAKE THE DOUGH, combine the cream cheese and butter in a large bowl. With a wooden spoon or electric mixer set on medium speed, beat until smooth. Stir in the vanilla.

SIFT together the flour, confectioners' sugar, and salt onto a piece of waxed paper. Gradually add to the cream cheese mixture, stirring just until all of the ingredients are evenly mixed.

DIVIDE the dough into 6 equal portions and shape each portion into a flat disk 5 inches in diameter. Cover with plastic wrap and refrigerate for 1 hour, or until firm.

TO MAKE THE FILLING, combine the walnuts, apricots, sugar, chocolate morsels, and cinnamon in a food processor. Pulse until the mixture is finely chopped and homogenous. Set aside.

PREHEAT the oven to 350°. Line 2 baking sheets with parchment paper.

(continued)

DOUGH

- $1/2$ pound cream cheese, at room temperature
- 1 cup (2 sticks) unsalted butter, at room temperature
- 1 teaspoon vanilla extract
- $2^2/_3$ cups unbleached all-purpose flour
- $1/4$ cup confectioners' sugar
- $1/4$ teaspoon salt

FILLING

- 1 cup walnuts
- $1/2$ cup dried apricots
- $1/2$ cup sugar
- $1/2$ cup semisweet chocolate morsels
- 3 tablespoons ground cinnamon

FINISHING THE COOKIES

- 6 tablespoons granulated sugar
- 2 teaspoons ground cinnamon
- 1 egg beaten with 2 teaspoons water

IN A SMALL BOWL, stir together the 6 tablespoons granulated sugar and 2 teaspoons cinnamon until well mixed. Reserve about 2 tablespoons of the cinnamon sugar. Sprinkle the remainder evenly on the prepared baking sheets.

REMOVE 1 dough disk from the refrigerator and roll it out on a lightly floured surface into a 10-inch round. Spread $1/2$ cup of the filling evenly over the dough. Press it into the dough by firmly rolling over it with the rolling pin. With a knife or a pizza cutter, divide the round into 12 wedges. Starting at the outer edge of the circle, roll up each wedge toward the center and curve the ends inward to form a crescent. Place the shaped cookies on the prepared baking sheets, spacing 1 inch apart and with the rolled tips on the bottom. Repeat with the remaining dough disks. Brush the crescents with the beaten egg and sprinkle with the reserved cinnamon sugar.

BAKE the cookies for 20 to 25 minutes, until slightly puffed and golden brown on the bottom. Let the cookies cool on the baking sheets on racks for 2 to 3 minutes; then carefully transfer to racks to cool. Store the cookies in a tightly closed tin. They taste best if eaten within a few days.

molasses CRACKLES

▶ MAKES ABOUT 4 DOZEN COOKIES

These are old-fashioned, perfectly round, soft cookies with a crackly top and plenty of spice—good comfort food to give any time of year. You should be able to find Sucanat (granulated dried cane juice) and turbinado sugar at a natural food store. If not, make the cookies anyway with the suggested substitutions.

IN A MIXING BOWL, combine the butter and Sucanat. With a wooden spoon or an electric mixer set on medium speed, beat until well combined. Add the molasses and eggs and mix until evenly blended.

SIFT together the flour, baking soda, salt, cinnamon, ginger, and cloves onto a piece of waxed paper. Add to the butter mixture, stirring until all of the ingredients are evenly mixed. Cover the bowl. Chill for 1 hour in the refrigerator.

PREHEAT the oven to 350°. Lightly butter baking sheets or line with parchment paper.

SPREAD the turbinado sugar on a saucer. Form the dough into walnut-sized balls (about 1 rounded tablespoon) and roll them in the sugar, coating evenly. Place them 3 inches apart on the prepared baking sheets.

BAKE the cookies for 12 to 15 minutes, until crackly and firm at the edges and still slightly soft in the middle. Let the cookies cool on the baking sheets on racks for 2 to 3 minutes, then carefully transfer them to the racks to cool. They will keep for about a week in a tightly closed tin.

1 cup (2 sticks) unsalted butter, at room temperature

$1^{1}/_{4}$ cup Sucanat (dried cane juice) or firmly packed brown sugar

1 cup dark molasses

2 eggs

$3^{1}/_{2}$ cups unbleached all-purpose flour

1 tablespoon plus 1 teaspoon baking soda

1 teaspoon salt

1 teaspoon ground cinnamon

1 teaspoon ground ginger

$1^{1}/_{2}$ teaspoons ground cloves

About $^{1}/_{2}$ cup turbinado or granulated sugar

triple-chocolate WALNUT COOKIES

▶ MAKES ABOUT 4 DOZEN COOKIES

Linda Kucera, chef and kind soul, supplied these cookies to my friend Patty regularly, and Patty kept them in her freezer. Patty and I would eat them surreptitiously while our children napped. Give these to a mother to eat on the sly or to share with the rest of the family. They have the satisfying chocolatey character of a brownie, yet maintain their integrity as cookies.

2 ounces unsweetened chocolate, chopped

1 ounce bittersweet chocolate, chopped

1 cup (2 sticks) unsalted butter, at room temperature

$^1/_2$ cup firmly packed light brown sugar

$^3/_4$ cup granulated sugar

2 eggs

2 teaspoons water

2$^1/_4$ cups unbleached all-purpose flour

1 teaspoon baking soda

1 teaspoon salt

3 tablespoons unsweetened cocoa powder

1 (6-ounce) package semisweet mini chocolate morsels

1 cup coarsely chopped walnuts

PREHEAT the oven to 350°. Lightly butter baking sheets or line with parchment paper.

COMBINE the unsweetened and bittersweet chocolates in a heatproof bowl and place over (not touching) hot water until melted. Stir until smooth and set aside.

COMBINE the butter and brown and granulated sugars in a mixing bowl. With a wooden spoon or an electric mixer set on medium speed, beat until creamy. Add the eggs and water and stir until well combined.

SIFT together the flour, baking soda, salt, and cocoa powder onto a piece of waxed paper. Add to the egg mixture one half at a time, mixing well after each addition. Stir in the melted chocolate until evenly mixed. Add the chocolate morsels and walnuts and stir only to combine. Do not overmix. Drop the dough by rounded teaspoonfuls onto the prepared baking sheets, spacing them 2 inches apart.

BAKE the cookies for 10 minutes. They will look puffed and still be slightly soft, almost underdone. (It's impossible to tell if they've browned because the cookie dough is so dark, but for these cookies it's better to err on the side of being underdone.)

LET the cookies cool on the baking sheets on racks for 2 to 3 minutes, then carefully transfer to the racks to cool. The cookies will keep for about a week in a tightly closed tin, or they can be well wrapped and frozen for up to 2 months.

coconut DREAM BARS

▶ MAKES 18 BARS

(pictured, page 120)

It's good to have a few recipes for bars in your back pocket. They're quick to put together. For easy cutting, wait until the baked sheet is cool, then slide it out of the pan, still on the parchment, onto a cutting board and slice with a heavy knife.

BOTTOM LAYER

1¹/₂ cups unbleached all-purpose flour

6 tablespoons firmly packed light or dark brown sugar

¹/₂ teaspoon salt

¹/₂ cup (1 stick) unsalted butter, chilled, cut into 1-inch pieces

1 teaspoon vanilla extract

TOP LAYER

2 eggs

1¹/₄ cups firmly packed dark brown sugar

1 tablespoon all-purpose flour

1 teaspoon baking powder

1 teaspoon vanilla extract

¹/₂ teaspoon salt

1 cup coarsely chopped walnuts

1 cup unsweetened flaked coconut

³/₄ cup dried cranberries

PREHEAT the oven to 350°. Butter the sides of a 9 by 13-inch baking pan and line the bottom with parchment paper.

TO MAKE THE BOTTOM LAYER, combine the flour, brown sugar, and salt in a food processor and process until well blended. Add the butter and process until the ingredients are evenly combined and the mixture looks crumbly but not dry. You want to stop short of allowing the dough to form a ball. Add the vanilla and pulse to mix. (If you don't have a food processor, use your fingers, a whisk, or the paddle attachment of a heavy-duty mixer.) Spread the crumbs evenly over the bottom of the prepared pan and press gently to firm them.

BAKE for 10 to 12 minutes, until golden. Remove from the oven.

TO MAKE THE TOP LAYER, beat the eggs in a bowl with a whisk until frothy. Add the brown sugar, flour, baking powder, vanilla, and salt and whisk until well combined. Stir in the walnuts, coconut, and cranberries and spread over the top of the baked bottom layer.

RETURN the pan to the oven for 20 to 22 minutes, or until golden brown. Transfer to a rack and let cool completely in the pan. Run a knife around the inside edge of the pan to loosen the baked sheet and carefully slide the whole thing, still on the parchment, onto a cutting board. Cut into 18 bars, each measuring about 2 inches by 3 inches. Carefully lift the bars from the parchment. The bars will keep for 3 to 4 days in a tightly closed tin.

chocolate-pecan **BARS**

▶ MAKES 18 BARS

Chewy and sweet, these treats are a cross between a candy and a bar. You may want to cut the bars in half on the diagonal to make triangles. And then again, you may just want to go for broke and present them whole.

BOTTOM LAYER

- 1½ cups unbleached all-purpose flour
- 6 tablespoons firmly packed light or dark brown sugar
- ½ teaspoon salt
- ½ cup (1 stick), chilled unsalted butter, cut into 1-inch pieces
- 1 teaspoon vanilla extract

TOP LAYER

- ½ cup (1 stick) unsalted butter
- ½ cup firmly packed light or dark brown sugar
- ½ cup dark corn syrup
- 1 tablespoon heavy whipping cream
- 1 teaspoon vanilla extract
- ⅛ teaspoon salt
- 2 ounces unsweetened chocolate, chopped into small pieces
- Finely grated zest of 1 large orange (about 1 tablespoon)
- 2 cups coarsely chopped pecans

PREHEAT the oven to 350°. Butter the sides of a 9 by 13-inch baking pan and line the bottom with parchment paper.

TO MAKE THE BOTTOM LAYER, combine the flour, brown sugar, and salt in a food processor and process until well blended. Add the butter and process until the ingredients are evenly combined and the mixture looks crumbly but not dry. You want to stop short of allowing the dough to form a ball. Add the vanilla and pulse to mix. (If you don't have a food processor, use your fingers, a whisk, or the paddle attachment of a heavy-duty mixer.) Spread the crumbs evenly over the bottom of the prepared pan and press gently to firm them.

BAKE for 10 to 12 minutes, until golden. Remove from the oven.

TO MAKE THE TOP LAYER, combine the butter, brown sugar, corn syrup, cream, vanilla, and salt in a heavy-bottomed saucepan. Stir over medium heat to melt the butter, then increase the heat and bring to a boil. Boil gently without stirring for 1 minute. Remove from the heat and add the chocolate, stirring until melted. Stir in the orange zest and pecans. Spread the topping over the baked bottom layer.

RETURN the pan to the oven and bake for 20 to 25 minutes, or until the topping is uniformly bubbly. Transfer to a rack and let cool completely in the pan. Run a knife around the inside edge of the pan to loosen the baked sheet and carefully slide the whole thing, still on the parchment, onto a cutting board. Cut into 18 bars, each measuring about 2 inches by 3 inches. Carefully lift the bars from the parchment. The bars will keep for 4 to 5 days stored between layers of waxed paper in a tightly closed tin.

BAR COOKIES MAKE GREAT GIFTS

Not only are bars quick and easy to make, but they also stack nicely and neatly in cellophane bags. Tied with a pretty ribbon, a bag of bars makes a great holiday gift for the folks in your neighborhood.

FAVORITE COOKIE-BAKING EQUIPMENT

- Inexpensive, heavy-duty aluminum baking sheets with 1-inch sides, (aka jelly-roll pans)
- Sturdy metal cooling racks, preferably large and with feet
- Parchment paper
- Long offset metal spatula (with a bend in it near the handle) for sliding underneath cookie dough
- Tablespoon-sized ice-cream scoop for drop cookies

OVERBAKED COOKIES

When cookies come out of the oven on the verge of burning, they can sometimes be saved. Transfer them quickly off the hot pan onto a rack. The air circulating under the cookies cools them quickly and keeps them crisp.

(continued on page 131)

maple-nut BARS

▶ MAKES 36 BARS

If you like your nuts without chocolate, these bars are a good choice. The slightly salty cashews add a pleasant surprise to this always-appreciated gift.

BOTTOM LAYER

3 cups unbleached all-purpose flour

¹/₂ cup firmly packed light or dark brown sugar

1 teaspoon salt

1 cup (2 sticks) unsalted butter, cut into 1-inch pieces

1 teaspoon vanilla extract

TOP LAYER

¹/₄ cup (¹/₂ stick) unsalted butter

¹/₂ cup pure maple syrup

¹/₄ cup light corn syrup

¹/₃ cup firmly packed dark brown sugar

1 teaspoon vanilla extract

²/₃ cup sliced almonds

²/₃ cup unblanched whole almonds

²/₃ cup lightly salted cashews

PREHEAT the oven to 350°. Butter the sides of a 13 by 18-inch jelly-roll pan and line the bottom with parchment paper.

TO MAKE THE BOTTOM LAYER, combine the flour, brown sugar, and salt together in a food processor and process until well blended. Add the butter and process until the ingredients are evenly combined and the mixture looks crumbly but not dry. You want to stop short of allowing the dough to form a ball. Add the vanilla and pulse to mix. (If you don't have a food processor, use your fingers, a whisk, or the paddle attachment of a heavy-duty mixer.) Spread the crumbs evenly over the bottom of the prepared pan and press gently to firm them.

BAKE for 10 to 12 minutes, until golden. Remove from the oven.

TO MAKE THE TOP LAYER, combine the butter, maple syrup, corn syrup, brown sugar, and vanilla in a heavy-bottomed saucepan. Stir over medium heat to melt the butter, then increase the heat and bring to a boil. Boil gently without stirring for 1 minute.

MIX together the nuts. Spread the topping over the baked bottom layer. Sprinkle the nuts on top. Return the pan to the oven and bake for about 18 minutes, or until the topping is uniformly bubbly and a deep, golden brown. Transfer to a rack and let cool completely in the pan. Run a knife around the inside edge of the pan to loosen the baked sheet and carefully slide the whole thing, still on the parchment, onto a cutting board. Cut into 36 bars, each measuring about 2 inches by 3 inches. Carefully lift the bars from the parchment. The bars will keep for 4 to 5 days between layers of waxed paper in a tightly closed tin.

QUANTITY BAKING

For marathon holiday baking, divide up the tasks: Mix several doughs on one night, bake them over the next few nights, and then wrap them all on the following night. Add about 5 minutes to the baking time if the cookie dough has been chilled and that step has not been called for in the recipe.

TIMING IS EVERYTHING

Never turn your back on a batch of cookies in the oven. You can talk on the phone, but set the timer and don't leave the kitchen. Check the cookies often and go primarily by the signs of doneness, not the time, to compensate for the inevitable quirks of individual ovens.

confections

chapter nine

The Candy Box

Christmas and Valentine's Day are traditionally the times we allow ourselves sweet indulgences. So if we're going to indulge, let's indulge in style! Fresh homemade candies have a special charm and cannot to be compared to what sits on store shelves for months. An elegant box of fruit jellies will impress your hosts and perhaps inspire them to share them with their guests along with dessert. Then again, they may choose to enjoy them later in calm solitude. Help pull a friend out of slump with a surprise package of your chocolates and a good novel. Whatever the occasion, homemade candy is a rare treat.

Although a simple tin or a pretty jar to hold your gift will suffice, candy lends itself to a classy presentation. Cake-decorating supply stores and craft stores are great sources of supplies and inspiration. Look for small candy cups, doilies, white cardboard chocolate boxes, and thin, gold elastic cord. Line the boxes with colored tissue, shiny foil wrap, or your favorite fancy wrapping paper. Be sure to put a barrier of waxed paper or cellophane between the candy and colored or metallic paper. Tie plain white boxes with fine gold or silver cord or with a wide, diaphanous ribbon, and tie on a trinket or a millinery decoration. Or you can wrap the entire box in beautiful paper.

Plain or lace cellophane bags from party supply stores or from cake-decorating supply stores make easy gift packages. So do brandy snifters, coffee mugs, odd bowls, plates, or sauceboats from an antique store. Look around a candy store or a gourmet shop for ideas, too.

marzipan-stuffed DATES and PRUNES

▶ MAKES 60 TO 70 CANDIES

These candies are relatively simple to make, yet are both unusual and beautiful. Present them in white paper candy cups in a box lined with colored tissue, or on an ornate china plate wrapped in clear cellophane. Be sure to look for good-quality almond paste, such as Odense brand. Do not confuse it with marzipan.

1 (7-ounce) tube almond paste

1²/₃ cups confectioners' sugar, or as needed

1 teaspoon freshly squeezed lemon juice

2 to 3 tablespoons light corn syrup

Red and green food coloring

1 to 2 tablespoons dark, fragrant rum, such as Myers's

1 to 2 tablespoons kirsch

30 to 35 dates

30 to 35 pitted prunes

TO MAKE THE MARZIPAN, break the almond paste into 1-inch pieces and combine it with the 1²/₃ cups confectioners' sugar in a food processor. Pulse until finely mixed and sandy looking. Add the lemon juice and 2 tablespoons of the corn syrup and pulse just until ingredients are combined. The mixture will look crumbly and slightly damp. Remove 1 tablespoon and test to see if it can be pressed together to form a smooth mass. If the mixture is too dry, add a little more corn syrup. If it is too sticky, add more confectioners' sugar.

TURN out the mixture onto a flat work surface, press it together, and knead it briefly until smooth. (Wrap in plastic and refrigerate if not using immediately. It can be stored this way for several months.)

DIVIDE the marzipan in half. To one half, add a few drops of green food coloring and rum to taste, kneading with your hands until the mixture is homogenous. Color the second half with red food coloring and flavor it with kirsch.

TO STUFF THE FRUITS, make a slit in the top of each date and remove the pit. Form a small piece of green marzipan ($^1/_2$ to $^3/_4$ teaspoon) into a sausage shape. Spread the date open along the slit, fill with the marzipan, and press the edges together to firm it into place. To decorate, use the back of a paring knife to make a vertical line down the middle and a series of short slanted lines on either side of the middle line to make a leaf pattern.

MAKE a small indentation in the middle of each prune. Form a small piece of pink marzipan ($^1/_2$ to $^3/_4$ teaspoon) into an oval shape and press it into the center of each prune. Draw the sides of the prune up around the marzipan to firm it into place. To decorate, use the back of a paring knife to make a trellis (crisscross) design.

STORE the candies between layers of waxed paper in a tightly closed tin for up to 10 days.

black currant FRUIT JELLIES

▶ MAKES 64 CANDIES

European candy shops offer a wonderful selection of fruit jellies, small colorful square jewels packed with concentrated tart fruit essence. They are hard to find in this country, and when you do find them, they're usually tired and flat. The candies look pretty in white paper cases on a decorative plate salvaged at a flea market. You might instead spread them on a large plate or stack them in a pyramid on a small one and wrap in cellophane. White candy boxes and small tins are other easy and attractive packaging options.

For the firmest jellies, use apple pectin powder, such as Vitpris brand from France (see Sources, page 162). You can also use Certo liquid pectin. The jellies will be slightly softer if made with Certo, but they will still be packed with flavor. Look for black currant syrup (used to make fruit drinks) in a gourmet food store or health food store. Ribena is a widely available brand.

¹/₄ cup apple pectin powder or 1 (6-ounce) package (2 pouches) or 1 (6-ounce) bottle Certo liquid pectin

2 cups sugar, plus additional sugar for coating

1 cup crème de cassis (black currant liqueur)

³/₄ cup black currant syrup

¹/₂ cup fruity red wine

1 tablespoon freshly squeezed lemon juice

CUT two 8 by 13-inch rectangles out of parchment paper to line an 8-inch square pan. Fit a piece of the parchment in the pan, creasing it at the two edges when it extends beyond the bottom. Place the second piece of parchment over it, in the opposite direction, so that the bottom and all four sides of the pan are fitted with paper.

COMBINE the apple pectin powder with ¹/₄ cup of the sugar and set aside. If you are using Certo, skip to the next step, using the full 2 cups sugar.

COMBINE the remaining sugar, crème de cassis, black currant syrup, wine, and lemon juice in a saucepan and bring to a boil over medium heat. Boil for 3 minutes, stirring to dissolve the sugar.

REMOVE the pan from the heat and stir in the pectin-sugar mixture or the Certo, mixing until thoroughly combined. Return the pan to the heat and bring to a boil, stirring constantly. Stir and boil for 1 minute if using Certo, for 4 minutes if using apple pectin powder. Pour into the prepared pan and let cool until set. The jelly may take several hours to set.

WHEN THE JELLY HAS SET, lift it out of the pan, using the parchment paper as handles, and lay it on a cutting board. Cut into 1-inch squares. Spread the additional sugar on a saucer and roll the jellies in the sugar to coat evenly. Store in a tightly closed tin in a cool place for 2 days. If longer storage is desired, do not cut the jelly into squares. Instead, wrap the uncut jelly in parchment paper, then wrap tightly in aluminum foil and store in the refrigerator for up to 6 weeks. Unwrap the jelly and blot with a paper towel if necessary. Cut and roll in sugar before packaging.

MAKING FRUIT JELLIES OF DIFFERING FLAVORS

Fruit jellies are so easy to make that you have to wonder why they are not more popular. They invite numerous variations: pear, peach, apricot, raspberry, kiwi fruit—you name it. Substitute 2 cups fresh fruit purée for the fruit and liquid in the recipes for black currant and cranberry jellies, and include a tablespoon or two of freshly squeezed lemon juice to enhance the fruit.

cranberry JELLIES

▶ MAKES 64 CANDIES

These jellies are delicious simply rolled in sugar, but for a truly wonderful treat, dip them in tempered bittersweet chocolate. The soft, tart cranberries make a stunning contrast to the outer crunch of dark chocolate.

1 Meyer lemon, or $^1/_2$ large regular lemon

1 (12-ounce) package of cranberries, picked over

$^1/_4$ cup water

$^1/_4$ cup apple pectin powder or 1 (6-ounce) package or 1 (6-ounce) bottle Certo liquid pectin

$2^1/_2$ cups sugar, plus additional sugar for coating

CUT two 8 by 13-inch rectangles out of parchment paper to line an 8-inch square pan. Fit a piece of the parchment in the pan, creasing it at two edges where it extends beyond the bottom. Place the second piece of parchment over it, in the opposite direction, so that the bottom and all four sides of the pan are fitted with paper.

SLICE the lemon in $^1/_4$-inch-thick slices, removing the seeds, and place in a food processor. Add the cranberries and water and purée until smooth. If you like a slightly chunky texture, stop before the mixture is very finely chopped.

COMBINE the apple pectin powder with $^1/_4$ cup of the sugar and set aside. If you are using Certo, skip to the next step, using the full $2^1/_2$ cups sugar.

COMBINE the cranberry purée and the remaining sugar in a saucepan and bring to a boil over medium heat. Boil for 4 minutes, stirring to dissolve sugar.

REMOVE the pan from the heat and stir in the pectin and sugar mixture or the Certo, mixing until thoroughly combined. Return the pan to the heat and bring to a boil. Stir and boil for 1 minute if using Certo, for 4 minutes if using apple pectin powder. Pour into the prepared pan and let cool until set. The jelly may take several hours to set.

(continued)

TO TEMPER CHOCOLATE

Tempering chocolate is accomplished in three steps: Completely melt the chocolate, cool it, and then rewarm it slightly to the correct temperature. Untempered chocolate looks streaky and dull, a far cry from the glossy finish desired for dipped or molded candies. Tempering chocolate takes patience and precision, but armed with an accurate chocolate thermometer, it is not out of reach for the home cook.

1. Put two thirds of the chocolate to be tempered in a stainless-steel or other heatproof bowl. Place over (not touching) hot water in a saucepan until melted. If a preferred melting temperature for tempering is not listed on the package, melt dark chocolate to between 120° and 125°, and milk and white chocolate to about 115°.

2. Cool the chocolate to 82° for dark chocolate, 79° for milk and white chocolate, by finely chopping the remaining chocolate and adding it a few tablespoons at a time, stirring after each addition, until the pieces are completely melted. Keep adding and stirring, and when the chocolate cools to the desired temperature, stop. The chopped

(continued on page 142)

WHEN THE JELLY HAS SET, lift it out of the pan, using the parchment paper as handles, and lay it on a cutting board. Cut into 1-inch squares. Spread the additional sugar on a saucer and roll the jellies in the sugar to coat evenly. Store in a tightly closed tin in a cool place for 2 days. If longer storage is desired, do not cut the jelly into squares. Instead, wrap the uncut jelly in parchment paper, then wrap tightly in aluminum foil and store in the refrigerator for up to 6 weeks. Unwrap the jelly and blot with a paper towel if necessary. Cut and roll in sugar before packaging.

BUTTERCRUNCH

▶ MAKES 2 ¹/₂ POUNDS CANDY

Buttercrunch is down-home candy. Over the years, I've gotten more requests for this recipe than any other. You could make more than one version, varying them with milk or white chocolate, hazelnuts, macadamias, or other toasted nuts. My favorite way to package these candies is in clear or lace cellophane bags tied up with a pretty ribbon.

You will need a candy thermometer to get the bottom layer of toffee just right. Be careful not to burn your fingers—300° is very hot—and be sure to use a metal implement to spread the toffee (plastic will melt). An offset spatula is ideal. Tempered chocolate looks beautiful and shiny on top of the toffee, but if you don't want to fuss with tempering, sprinkle a few more nuts on top to disguise the less than perfect chocolate underneath. The candy will taste just as good!

(pictured, page 148, right)

1 pound good-quality unsalted butter

2 cups sugar

1 tablespoon light corn syrup

1 teaspoon vanilla extract

1 cup chopped walnuts

8 ounces bittersweet chocolate, chopped

LINE a 13 by 18-inch baking sheet, preferably with a 1-inch rim, with parchment paper.

COMBINE the butter, sugar, corn syrup, and vanilla in a heavy-bottomed 4-quart saucepan. Place over medium to high heat and heat, stirring with a long-handled wooden spoon, until the mixture comes to a boil and reaches 300° on a candy thermometer.

REMOVE the pan from the heat and stir in half of the chopped walnuts. Immediately pour the mixture onto the parchment-lined sheet and spread to the corners and edges with a metal spatula.

LET COOL for 10 minutes. Blot with a paper towel to remove any excess butter that may have risen to the surface. Let cool completely.

(continued)

chocolate you add must be in a tempered state, that is, from the original package and not previously melted.

3. Rewarm the chocolate. Place the bowl over (not touching) hot water and stir until the dark chocolate reaches 88° to 91° and white and milk chocolate reach 87° to 89°

4. Do a test before you proceed. Thinly spread a spoonful on a piece of parchment or waxed paper and put it in the refrigerator for about 2 minutes. It should set quickly, be shiny, and snap nicely when broken. If not, you must start over and reheat the chocolate to the required temperature. Go back to step 1 and add more chopped chocolate, fresh from the package, as directed in step 2.

5. Hold your temper. To keep the chocolate within the correct temperature range while you dip, place the bowl on a heating pad set at low heat. If the temperature starts to rise, set a pot holder or a folded dish towel under the bowl of chocolate. Stir the chocolate often. It is easier to keep a large amount of chocolate tempered, so temper more than you need. Unused chocolate can be poured onto a piece of parchment to harden and stored for later use.

MELT the chocolate in a stainless-steel or other heatproof bowl over (not touching) hot water and temper it if you prefer. Spread the chocolate over the cooled toffee and sprinkle with the remaining nuts. Let cool until firm, then break into pieces.

STORE the pieces between sheets of waxed paper in a tightly closed tin in a cool place (not the refrigerator) for up to 2 weeks.

MENDIANTS

▶ MAKES ABOUT 28 CANDIES

These pretty coin-shaped candies are in every confiserie *window in Belgium. They were originally made with almonds, raisins, hazelnuts, and figs, to symbolize the colors of the four Roman Catholic mendicant orders. Pistachios, pecans, walnuts, dried papaya pieces, golden raisins, dried pineapple pieces—whatever strikes your fancy—can be added to the traditional fruits and nuts. Use dark, milk, or white chocolate, or prepare an assortment of all three. The candies are simple to make, and a friend will feel rich indeed to receive a package of these "beggars."*

1 cup mixed dried fruits and nuts

9 ounces bittersweet, milk, or white chocolate, tempered (page 140)

PREHEAT the oven to 350°.

CUT the fruits into $^1/_4$-inch pieces. Spread the nuts on a baking sheet and toast in the oven for up to 15 minutes, or until fragrant. Let cool and break into pieces if very large.

LINE a baking sheet with parchment paper. Spoon the chocolate onto the parchment with a tablespoon or soupspoon to make 2-inch disks. Sprinkle the fruit and nuts over the chocolate disks and let stand in a cool place to set. This will take 10 to 20 minutes.

STORE the candies between layers of waxed paper in a tightly closed tin in a cool place (not the refrigerator) for up to 2 weeks.

almond ROCHERS

▶ MAKES ABOUT 3 DOZEN

These little boulders can also be made with other toasted nuts such as chopped walnuts, hazelnut, or pecan pieces or even with shredded coconut. If you don't want to fuss with tempering, melt the chocolate, mix it with the nuts, spoon the mixture into little brown petit-four cases, and sprinkle with finely chopped toasted nuts before the chocolate is completely set. Note that the recipe uses slivered, as opposed to sliced, almonds.

2 cups slivered blanched almonds

8 ounces dark chocolate, tempered (page 140)

PREHEAT the oven to 350°. Spread the almonds on a baking sheet and toast them in the oven for 8 to 10 minutes, until light brown and slightly fragrant. Let cool.

LINE a baking sheet with parchment or waxed paper for the finished candies.

In a bowl, combine the almonds with half of the tempered chocolate and mix with a rubber spatula until the nuts are thoroughly coated. Add the remaining chocolate and mix to coat again.

WORKING quickly so that the chocolate doesn't set, spoon little mounds of the mixture onto the parchment-lined pan. Use 2 teaspoons, one to scoop and the other to scrape the mixture onto the pan. Let stand at cool room temperature until set. This will take 10 to 20 minutes.

STORE the candies between layers of waxed paper in a tightly closed tin in a cool place (not the refrigerator) for up to 3 weeks.

chocolate **BARK**

At its most basic, chocolate bark is simply tempered chocolate spread on a sheet of parchment that is left to harden and then broken into pieces. It's a good use for any tempered chocolate that remains after dipping candy centers, or it can be an end in itself. The bark can be thick or thin, according to your preference, and it can add a nice touch to a candy assortment.

Using an offset spatula, spread tempered chocolate (page 140) on a piece of parchment and let it harden at room temperature. You can make a pattern with a decorator's comb while the chocolate is still soft, or sprinkle it with toasted sliced almonds or other nuts. When it is completely hard, break it into irregular pieces.

You can also combine the tempered chocolate with other ingredients before spreading. To 12 ounces tempered white, milk, or dark chocolate, add about 2 cups of one of the following: toasted slivered blanched almonds; toasted walnut pieces; raisins; skinned, chopped, and toasted hazelnuts; toasted pecan pieces; or toasted coconut. Spread the chocolate to a thickness of $^1/_8$ inch, making sure the nuts or other additions are evenly distributed. Rap the pan once or twice on the countertop to settle the chocolate, and let it harden at cool room temperature. Break into irregular pieces.

Store the bark between pieces of waxed paper in a tightly closed tin in a cool place (not the refrigerator) for up to 3 weeks.

mystery TRUFFLES

▶ MAKES 45 TO 50 CANDIES

(pictured, page 148, left)

I like the dark, bitter taste of unsweetened cocoa in contrast to the creamy inside of these truffles, and the whiskey gives them something mysterious, something je ne sais quoi.

Although Hershey's will do in a pinch, look for an imported cocoa whose deep, almost-ebony powder will give your truffles an irresistible appearance. Don't try to make small, perfectly round balls. These can be relatively large (2 bites) and misshapen, like the real thing—a fungus, after all. The recipe can be doubled or tripled.

The simplest way to gift wrap is to place the truffles in a pretty container: an oversized coffee cup or mug, a small flowerpot, even a large stemmed glass. Candy boxes lined with beautiful paper are also lovely.

CENTERS

12 ounces bittersweet chocolate, finely chopped (about 2 1/2 cups)

2/3 cup heavy whipping cream

1/4 cup (1/2 stick) unsalted butter, at room temperature, cut into 1-inch pieces

3 tablespoons whiskey

COATING

12 ounces bittersweet chocolate, finely chopped

About 1 cup sifted Dutch-process cocoa powder

TO MAKE THE CENTERS, place the chocolate in a heatproof bowl. Pour water to a depth of 2 inches into a saucepan that will accommodate the bottom of the bowl and bring to a boil. Turn off the heat.

BRING the cream to a simmer in a small saucepan (or in a Pyrex measuring cup in the microwave). Pour it over the chocolate in the bowl and, with a wooden spoon, begin stirring the cream and chocolate together in a small circle at the center of the bowl. When the mixture starts to look creamy at the center, very gradually widen the circle to incorporate all of the cream and chocolate. If bits of unmelted chocolate remain after all is stirred and creamy, place the bowl over the hot water in the saucepan and stir for 30 seconds. Remove and stir gently off the heat for another minute. Repeat once or twice more if necessary until the chocolate is completely melted.

ADD the butter and stir until smooth. Add the whiskey 1 tablespoon at a time, stirring after each addition until the liquid has been incorporated. Cover the bowl with plastic wrap and refrigerate for 45 to 60 minutes, until firm but not hard.

LINE a tray with parchment paper. When the mixture is firm, use a melon baller or small ice-cream scoop dipped in hot water to scoop up scant 1-inch balls. If necessary, shape after scooping with the tips of your fingers. Set the truffle centers on the parchment-lined tray and chill them in the refrigerator for 30 minutes.

PREHEAT the oven to 200°. Place a dinner plate in the oven to warm.

TO MAKE THE COATING, place the chocolate in a heatproof bowl placed over (not touching) hot water in a saucepan.

(continued)

LINE a baking sheet with parchment or waxed paper and sift a thin layer of cocoa over it.

POUR a shallow pool of the melted chocolate onto the warmed plate and place 5 or 6 truffle centers on top. With your outspread hand, roll the truffles in the chocolate in a circular motion to coat them with a thin layer of chocolate. Then carefully set them on the parchment-lined tray. Repeat with all the truffle centers. If the chocolate coating starts to harden from the cold centers, return the plate to the oven for 30 seconds to warm it.

GENEROUSLY SIFT cocoa over the truffles. Shake the pan to coat the truffles with the cocoa, sifting more cocoa over them if necessary.

WHEN the coating is completely set (10 to 20 minutes), store the truffles in a tightly closed tin in a cool place (not the refrigerator) for up to 10 days.

gifts for the host

chapter ten

Uncommon
Courtesy

find that I'm always racking my brain to come up with
enticing tidbits, beyond the ubiquitous cheese and crackers,
to offer guests with a glass of wine. Knowing that many of
my friends are in the same boat, I can be assured that a jar of olives with herbs
or of marinated goat cheese will be happily received. During the holidays, it's
especially handy to have a little something different in the pantry or the refrigerator to pull out at a moment's notice.

In this chapter you will find suggestions for savory gifts that are simple to
prepare and can be transported easily to a friend's house, for serving immediately or to put away for another day.

TAPENADE

What host wouldn't welcome an earthenware crock or a wide-mouthed jar of this Provençal olive paste? It makes a lively hors d'oeuvre to serve with drinks. It can be accompanied with crudités, hard-boiled eggs, or baguette slices, or it can be enjoyed the day after the party on a sandwich of crusty bread, goat cheese, and roasted peppers.

The recipe can be doubled or tripled if you're aiming for larger-scale production. Versions of this spread are numerous, so don't hesitate to vary the seasonings. The choice of olives will determine the flavor of the end result. If possible, ask the deli counterperson for a taste before buying. If the olives are not already pitted, bear in mind that you'll be doing that job. Choose large, meaty olives to save time and effort, or go the distance with smaller ones with irresistible character. Green olives have their own charm and can be substituted.

$1/2$ pound large black olives (about $1^1/2$ cups)

4 anchovy fillets, rinsed and patted dry

3 tablespoons capers

1 teaspoon finely chopped fresh thyme or savory

1 teaspoon finely grated lemon zest

Small pinch of freshly ground black pepper

$1/4$ cup good-quality olive oil

TO PIT THE OLIVES, place an olive flat on a cutting board, cover with the heel of one hand, place your other hand on top of the first one for added pressure, and bear down hard. The olive should crack open and the pit will be released. Place the pitted olives in a food processor.

ADD the anchovy fillets, capers, thyme, lemon zest, and salt to the processor and pulse to make a coarse purée. With the motor running, gradually add the olive oil, processing until you have a spreadable paste.

PACK the paste in a wide-mouthed half-pint jar or ceramic crock, cap tightly, and store in the refrigerator for up to several weeks.

herb-marinated **OLIVES**

► MAKES 1 PINT JAR

A pretty jar makes this gift special. French preserving jars with metal clasps are easy to find at housewares stores, or present the olives in an earthenware container with a lid. The long-keeping quality of these olives makes them especially suited to gift giving.

As with tapenade, the seasonings can be left to the discretion of the cook. I like the combination of orange, fennel, and rosemary in this mix, but you could omit them and accent the lemon and pepper instead, or add other woody herbs (soft herbs, like basil or parsley, don't keep well). Since garlic spoils easily, I don't use it unless the olives will be consumed within 1 or 2 days. Mixed sizes and colors of olives make a nice assortment, too. The recipe can be doubled or tripled to make several gifts.

(pictured, page 157, right)

2 cups olives in brine

$^1/_2$ orange

$^1/_2$ lemon

$^1/_2$ teaspoon whole black peppercorns

$^1/_2$ teaspoon fennel seeds

5 or 6 thyme sprigs

1 tablespoon coarsely chopped fresh rosemary

About 1 cup olive oil

DRAIN the olives and place them in a bowl.

SCRUB the rinds of the orange and lemon halves. If you have a citrus zester, use it to remove the zest of both the orange and lemon in pretty, thin slivers. Otherwise, remove the zest with a vegetable peeler and cut into fine julienne with a knife. Add it to the bowl of olives.

COMBINE the peppercorns and fennel in a mortar and very gently crush with a pestle. You just want to bruise them to release their flavor. Add to the olives.

RUB the thyme between your hands over the bowl of olives. Then add the rosemary. Turn the olives to coat them with the seasonings. Transfer the olives to a clean pint jar. Add enough olive oil to cover the olives, cover the jar, and refrigerate.

THE OLIVES will taste best after they have had a few days to absorb the flavors of the herbs. They will keep, refrigerated, for about 6 weeks. Olive oil often coagulates in the refrigerator, however, so allow the jar to come to room temperature before serving.

goat cheese ROUNDS in HERBS and OLIVE OIL

▶ MAKES 1 LITER JAR

Friends have often requested these when I've asked what they would like me to bring for a weekend visit or a dinner party. Gift-tag suggestions could include spreading on baguette slices or crackers, serving in salad, or coating with bread crumbs and baking at 400° until warm, about 8 minutes.

These days it's not hard to find good domestic goat cheese logs in most supermarkets. The shape makes it ideal for slicing into "buttons" and marinating. The choice of herbs can be determined by the cook's preference, but garlic should be avoided because it does not store well. Use a fruity olive oil, something that you will enjoy tasting with the cheese.

2 small sprigs thyme

2 small sprigs savory

2 small sprigs rosemary

1 (10-ounce) or 2 (5-ounce) logs mild fresh goat cheese

1 teaspoon mixed whole peppercorns, in two or more colors (black, pink, white, or green)

$1/4$ teaspoon coriander seeds

2 or 3 bay leaves

About $1^1/_2$ cups olive oil

STERILIZE a wide-mouthed glass liter jar by immersing it in boiling water for 10 minutes. Drain and let dry thoroughly.

USING SCISSORS, snip the thyme, savory, and rosemary sprigs into lengths that will fit comfortably in the jar. Set aside. Cut the goat cheese into "buttons" about $1/2$ inch thick. To make neat cuts, use a knife dipped in hot water and wiped clean between each slice, or better yet, use a piece of dental floss (hold the mint!).

LAYER the cheese in the jar with the peppercorns, coriander seeds, and some of the herbs sprigs. Slip the bay leaves and 1 or 2 herb sprigs attractively against the sides of the jar as you layer. When the jar is full, pour in olive oil to cover the cheese completely, cover the jar, and refrigerate.

A JAR of marinated goat cheese will keep for as long as a month in the refrigerator. Olive oil often coagulates in the refrigerator, however, so allow the jar to come to room temperature before serving.

marinated EGGPLANT SPREAD

▶ MAKES 1 PINT JAR

The recipient of this aromatic spread may choose to serve it as an appetizer with garlic croutons to dinner guests, or save it for sandwiches later. Accompany the gift with a tag suggesting to spread it on slices of sourdough or French bread topped with a few basil leaves, tomato slices, and fresh mozzarella. Use a jar, a pretty bowl, a crock, or an earthenware dish for a container.

The vegetables can be grilled over a low flame outside if you don't want to turn on the oven on a hot day. I always make a double batch and keep half for myself.

1 large eggplant, about
    1^1/$_2$ pounds

Kosher salt

About ^{1}/$_4$ cup olive oil

1 small onion, quartered

^{1}/$_4$ cup chopped fresh basil

^{1}/$_4$ cup chopped fresh parsley

1 to 2 tablespoons balsamic
    vinegar

Salt

Freshly ground black pepper

TRIM the eggplant, but do not peel. Cut lengthwise into ^{1}/$_2$-inch-thick slices. Sprinkle the slices lightly with kosher salt and stand them in a colander to drain for 30 minutes.

MEANWHILE, preheat the oven to 500°. Line a baking sheet with aluminum foil and brush it with olive oil.

PAT the eggplant slices dry with paper towels and brush both sides of each slice with olive oil. Arrange the slices in a single layer on the foil-lined baking sheet. Brush the onion quarters with olive oil and place them on the baking sheet with the eggplant.

ROAST the vegetables, turning them once or twice, for 25 to 30 minutes, or until browned and tender. (The onions may take a few minutes longer than the eggplant.) Remove from the oven and let cool.

COARSELY CHOP the eggplant and onion and place in a bowl. Add the basil, parsley, and the vinegar, salt, and pepper to taste and stir to mix well. Taste and adjust the seasoning.

THE SPREAD will keep for about 1 week in a tightly closed container in the refrigerator. It can be served at room temperature or chilled.

smoked **FISH PÂTÉ**

(pictured, page 157, left)

▶ MAKES TWO 1-CUP RAMEKINS

For the friend who entertains a lot, here's a good appetizer to have on hand during the Christmas holidays. It goes together quickly, yet is elegant enough to serve with a glass of fine wine. Accompany your gift with some crackers. It's also good served with thinly sliced whole-grain bread.

In this recipe from Ireland, mackerel is the traditional choice of fish, but you could make it with other smoked fish, such as bluefish or trout. Look for smoked fish at the fish counter or in the deli section of your supermarket.

$^1/_2$ pound smoked mackerel fillets

$^1/_4$ cup ($^1/_2$ stick) unsalted butter, at room temperature

6 ounces ($^3/_4$ cup) cream cheese, at room temperature

Juice of $^1/_2$ lemon, or as needed

2 tablespoons finely chopped fresh parsley

1 tablespoon finely chopped fresh chives

Salt and coarsely ground black pepper

2 bay leaves

5 to 6 tablespoons clarified butter (see note)

REMOVE the skin from the mackerel fillets. Using a fork, flake the fish onto a plate, removing any errant bones.

IN A BOWL, beat together the butter and cream cheese until smooth. Stir in the flaked fish. Add the lemon juice, parsley, chives, and salt and pepper to taste. Taste and adjust the seasoning, adding more lemon juice if needed. Don't skimp on the black pepper.

PACK the fish mixture into two 1-cup ramekins. Smooth the tops of the ramekins until they are level. Place a bay leaf on top of each, cover with a thin layer of clarified butter, cover with plastic wrap, and refrigerate. The butter seals out air, allowing for a longer storage time. The spread will keep 4 to 5 days in the refrigerator. If you omit the butter, the spread will keep for 1 to 2 days.

Note: To clarify butter, melt butter (salted or unsalted, according to your preference) over medium heat and pour it into a glass measuring pitcher. Skim off and discard the surface foam, then carefully ladle off the clear butter into a separate container. Discard the milky solids at the bottom. The glass measuring cup isn't essential, but it makes it easier to see the various layers.

scottish OAT CAKES

▶ MAKES ABOUT 3 DOZEN CRACKERS

(pictured, page 157, center

Crumbly rather than crisp, these oat cakes offer a welcome change from the usual crackers. Pack them in an attractive tin and give them along with your favorite cheese or a ramekin of Smoked Fish Pâté (page 156). Or pair them with a jar of your homemade jam; they're pleasant for nibbling at teatime with butter and marmalade, too.

1¹/₂ cups old-fashioned rolled oats

¹/₂ cup unbleached all-purpose
    flour

¹/₂ cup whole-wheat flour

2 tablespoons wheat bran

2 teaspoons brown sugar

1 teaspoon baking powder

¹/₂ teaspoon salt

¹/₂ cup (1 stick) chilled unsalted but-
    ter, cut into 1-inch pieces

5 to 6 tablespoons milk

PREHEAT the oven to 350°. Butter a baking sheet or line with parchment paper.

IN A FOOD PROCESSOR, combine the rolled oats, all-purpose and whole-wheat flours, wheat bran, brown sugar, baking powder, and salt. Pulse briefly to mix and to chop the oats coarsely. Add the butter pieces and pulse again until evenly mixed. Add 5 tablespoons of the milk and pulse until the mixture starts to clump together.

EMPTY the contents of the processor bowl onto a work surface and press together to form a dough. Work in another tablespoon of milk if the dough is very crumbly. Divide the dough in half.

ROLL OUT one half of the dough on a lightly floured work surface to a thickness of ¹/₈ inch. Using a fluted 3-inch round cookie cutter, cut out rounds and arrange on the prepared baking sheet. Repeat with the remaining dough, including the scraps.

BAKE the crackers for 20 to 25 minutes, or until golden brown on the bottom. Transfer to a rack to cool. They will keep in a tightly closed tin for about 1 week.

Stilton Oat Cakes

These oat cakes are flavorful enough that they need no adornment. Partner them with a bottle of wine. Follow the recipe for Scottish Oat Cakes, but omit the sugar and add 2 ounces Stilton or other blue cheese, cut into small pieces, with the butter. If the cheese is strong, 2 ounces (or about $1/3$ cup small pieces) will be enough to impart a pleasantly cheesy taste. Use slightly more if you want a sharper flavor. You could cut the crackers into smaller rounds for one-bite snacks. They would be good made with grated sharp Cheddar, too.

sweet and salty TOASTED PECANS

▶ MAKES TWO 2-CUP PACKAGES

These are killers. Just try to keep your hand out of a bowl of them. You can note on the gift tag that they are great with cocktails or in a salad, but nobody needs an excuse to eat them. The two turns in the oven is what makes these nuts so crunchy and flavorful. Pack them in pretty jars, in cellophane bags tied with a ribbon, or in small ceramic bowls that friends can use again and again.

4 cups pecans halves

1¹/₂ cups water

3 cups sugar

2 tablespoons mild vegetable oil

2 teaspoons vanilla extract

1 teaspoon kosher salt

¹/₂ teaspoon ground cinnamon

¹/₄ teaspoon freshly ground black pepper

PREHEAT the oven to 325°. Line 2 baking sheets with aluminum foil and brush them lightly with vegetable oil.

COMBINE the pecans, water, and sugar in a saucepan and, stirring occasionally, bring to a boil over medium heat. Continue to boil, stirring occasionally, for 5 minutes.

REMOVE the nuts with a slotted spoon and spread them on the prepared baking sheets in a single layer. They should not be touching. Bake the nuts for 25 minutes, or until they turn a deep, toasty brown.

REMOVE the pans from the oven and let the nuts cool slightly. Leave the oven turned to 325°. Push the nuts into a mound in the center of each baking sheet, making sure the nuts are not stuck together.

DRIZZLE half of the oil and vanilla over each mound and toss to coat evenly.
In a small bowl, stir together the salt, cinnamon, and pepper until well mixed.
Sprinkle the mixture over the nuts, again using half for each baking pan. Toss
until the nuts are evenly coated with the spiced mixture.

SPREAD the nuts out in a single layer. Bake for 10 more minutes, or until
browned and crisp. Let cool completely. Store the nuts in an airtight container
at room temperature for up to 10 days.

Sources

New York Cake and Baking Distributor
56 West 22nd Street
New York, NY 10010
Telephone 1-800-94-CAKE-9

Over 100 pages of things you never knew you needed, including cellophane bags, plastic squeeze bottles, candy making and wrapping supplies, baking pans, parchment, dough scrapers, ice cream scoops, cookie cutters, and almond paste.

The Baker's Catalogue
King Arthur Flour
P.O. Box 876
Norwich, VT 05055-0876
Telephone 1-800-827-6836
Website www.kingarthurflour.com

A terrific resource for all your baking needs. Powdered buttermilk, baking pans, dough scrapers, vanilla beans, parchment, and much more.

Sur La Table
1765 Sixth Avenue South
Seattle, WA 98134-1608
Telephone 1-800-243-0852
Website www.surlatable.com

Chocolate tempering and candy thermometers, baking pans, canning jars, ramekins, paper loaf pans, and other good stuff.

Dean and Deluca
560 Broadway
New York, NY 10012
Telephone 1-800-221-7714
Website www.deandeluca.com

Spices, chiles, exotic teas, chocolate tempering thermometer, baking supplies, wine gift bags.

Williams-Sonoma
P.O. Box 7456
San Francisco, CA 94120-7456
Telephone 1-800-541-2233

Gift boxes, waxed tissue paper, holiday ribbon, decorating sugars and icing pens, candy boxes, candy cups, cellophane rolls.

Martha By Mail
P.O. Box 60060
Tampa, FL 33660-0060
Telephone 1-800-950-7130
Website www.marthabymail.com

Pressed glass jars, cookie cutters, cookie tins, cookie decorating kit, cellophane gift bags.

S.O.S. Chefs NYC
New York, NY
Telephone: 1-212-505-5813

Vitpris Ruban Noir powdered apple pectin for making fruit jellies.

Index

squeeze bottles for, 108
White Chocolate Icing, 108
Irish Whiskey Marmalade, 43

J

Jalapeños, Pickled, 82
Jams and marmalades. *See also* Preserved
    fruits
    Blackberry-Peach Jam, 33–34
    Blood Orange Marmalade, 42–43
    Blueberry-Raspberry Jam, 32
    boiling water bath for, 30–31
    Clementine-Cranberry Marmalade, 45
    End-of-Summer Jam, 40–41
    fruits for, 29–30
    as gifts, 31
    Irish Whiskey Marmalade, 43
    jars for, 30
    jellying point, 30–31
    Plum and Lemon Jam, 38–39
    storing, 31
    Strawberry Rubies, 35–36
Jars
    boiling water bath for, 30–31
    covers for, 10
    for jams, 30
    wide-mouthed, 58
Jellying point, 30–31

L

Labels, 5
Lavender-Lemon Tea Cakes, 96, 98
Lemons
    Blood Orange Marmalade, 42–43
    Blueberry-Lemon Sauce, 48
    Cherry and Apricot Compote, 57–58
    Clementine-Cranberry Marmalade, 45
    End-of-Summer Jam, 40–41
    Home-Canned Peaches in a Light
        Lemon Syrup, 49–50
    Lavender-Lemon Tea Cakes, 96, 98
    Plum and Lemon Jam, 38–39
    Preserved Lemons, 85, 87

Liqueurs
    Framboise, 65
    as gifts, 63–64
    Orange Ratafia, 67
    Plums in Plum Liqueur, 59, 61
    Strawberry Cordial, 70–71
    Sweet Blackberry Wine, 68

M

Mailing, 17
Maple-Cranberry Granola, 24
Maple-Nut Bars, 130–31
Marinated Eggplant Spread, 155
Marmalades. *See* Jams and marmalades
Marzipan-Stuffed Dates and Prunes,
    134–35
Mendiants, 143
Mexican-Style Hot-Chocolate Mix, 25
Molasses Crackles, 123
Muffin Mix, New England Corn-, 23
Mustard, Homemade Grainy, 88
Mystery Truffles, 146–49

N

New England Corn-Muffin Mix, 23
Nuts. *See also individual nuts*
    Maple-Nut Bars, 130–31
    Mendiants, 143

O

Oats
    Maple-Cranberry Granola, 24
    Scottish Oat Cakes, 158
    Stilton Oat Cakes, 159
Olives
    Herb-Marinated Olives, 153
    Tapenade, 152
Oranges
    Blood Orange Marmalade, 42–43
    Clementine-Cranberry Marmalade, 45
    Irish Whiskey Marmalade, 43
    Orange Buckwheat Pancake and
        Waffle Mix, 22
    Orange Ratafia, 67

Organization, 2–3
Ornaments
    Christmas cookie, 110
    on gifts, 5
Out-of-This-World Five-Grain Pancake
    and Waffle Mix, 20
Oven-Dried Tomatoes, 83–84

P

Palets de Dames, 112
Pancake and waffle mixes
    Orange Buckwheat Pancake and
        Waffle Mix, 22
    Out-of-This-World Five-Grain
        Pancake and Waffle Mix, 20
Paper, 4, 12–13
Pâté, Smoked Fish, 156
Peaches
    Blackberry-Peach Jam, 33–34
    End-of-Summer Jam, 40–41
    freezing, 34
    Home-Canned Peaches in a Light
        Lemon Syrup, 49–50
    Peaches in Raspberry Champagne,
        51, 53
    Red Tomato and Peach Chutney,
        89–90
Pears
    End-of-Summer Jam, 40–41
    Pears in Red Wine, 54, 56
Pecans
    Chocolate-Pecan Bars, 128–29
    Sweet and Salty Toasted Pecans,
        160–61
Pickles
    boiling water bath for, 30–31
    Green Cherry Tomato Pickles, 80
    Pickled Jalapeños, 82
Pinwheel Cookies, 116–17
Plums
    End-of-Summer Jam, 40–41
    Plum and Lemon Jam, 38–39
    Plums in Plum Liqueur, 59, 61